THE ACTING EDITION OF

The Royal Family

A COMEDY IN THREE ACTS

By

George S. Kaufman

and

Edna Ferber

SAMUEL FRENCH, INC.

45 West 25th Street NEW YORK, N.Y. 10010

7623 Sunset Boulevard HOLLYWOOD 90046

LONDON *TORONTO*

Copyright © 1927 by George S. Kaufman and Edna Ferber
Copyright © (Acting edition) 1929 by George S. Kaufman and Edna Ferber
Copyright © 1954 (In Renewal) by George S. Kaufman and Edna Ferber
Copyright © 1956 (In Renewal) by George S. Kaufman and Edna Ferber
Copyright © 1977 (Revised version) by Harriet Pilpel (as trustee under the will of Edna Ferber), Anne Kaufman Schneider and Leueen MacGrath

ALL RIGHTS RESERVED

CAUTION: Professionals and amateurs are hereby warned that THE ROYAL FAMILY is subject to a royalty. it is fully protected under the copyright laws of the United States of America, the British Commonwealth, including Canada, and all other countries of the Copyright Union. All rights, including professional, amateur, motion picture, recitation, lecturing, public reading, radio broadcasting, television, and the rights of translation into foreign languages are strictly reserved. In its present form the play is dedicated to the reading public only.

The amateur live stage performance rights to THE ROYAL FAMILY are controlled exclusively by Samuel French, Inc., and royalty arrangements and licenses must be secured well in advance of presentation. PLEASE NOTE that amateur royalty fees are set upon application in accordance with your producing circumstances. When applying for a royalty quotation and license please give us the number of performances intended, dates of production, your seating capacity and admission fee. Royalties are payable one week before the opening performance of the play to Samuel French, Inc., at 45 W. 25th Street, New York, NY 10010; or at 7623 Sunset Blvd., Hollywood, CA 90046, or to Samuel French (Canada), Ltd., 80 Richmond Street East, Toronto, Ontario, Canada M5C 1P1.

Royalty of the required amount must be paid whether the play is presented for charity or gain and whether or not admission is charged.

Stock royalty quoted on application to Samuel French, Inc.

For all other rights than those stipulated above, apply to Samuel French, Inc.

Particular emphasis is laid on the question of amateur or professional readings, permission and terms for which must be secured in writing from Samuel French, Inc.

Copying from this book in whole or in part is strictly forbidden by law, and the right of performance is not transferable.

Whenever the play is produced the following notice must appear on all programs, printing and advertising for the play: "Produced by special arrangement with Samuel French, Inc."

Due authorship credit must be given on all programs, printing and advertising for the play.

ISBN 0 573 61494 6 Printed in U.S.A

No one shall commit or authorize any act or omission by which the copyright of, or the right to copyright, this play may be impaired.

No one shall make any changes in this play for the purpose of production.

Publication of this play does not imply availability for performance. Both amateurs and professionals considering a production are *strongly* advised in their own interests to apply to Samuel French, Inc., for written permission before starting rehearsals, advertising, or booking a theatre.

No part of this book may be reproduced, stored in a retrieval system, or transmitted in any form, by any means, now known or yet to be invented, including mechanical, electronic, photocopying, recording, videotaping, or otherwise, without the prior written permission of the publisher.

The following is a copy of program of the first performance of "THE ROYAL FAMILY," as presented at the Selwyn Theatre, New York, N. Y., December 28th, 1927:

JED HARRIS

Presents

THE ROYAL FAMILY

A Comedy in Three Acts

By

George S. Kaufman and Edna Ferber

Staged by David Burton

THE CAST

(In the order of their first appearance)

DELLA .... *Josephine Williams*
JO .... *Royal C. Stout*
HALLBOY .... *Wally Stuart*
MCDERMOTT .... *Murray Alper*
HERBERT DEAN .... *Orlando Daly*
KITTY DEAN .... *Catherine Calhoun-Doucet*
GWEN .... *Sylvia Field*
PERRY STEWART .... *Roger Pryor*
FANNY CAVENDISH .... *Haidee Wright*
OSCAR WOLFE .... *Jefferson de Angelis*
JULIE CAVENDISH .... *Ann Andrews*
ANTHONY CAVENDISH .... *Otto Kruger*
ANOTHER HALLBOY .... *Lester Neilson*
GILBERT MARSHALL .... *Joseph King*
GUNGA .... *Hubert Courtney*
MISS PEAKE .... *Phyllis Rose*
CHAUFFEUR .... *Frank Volimer*

The action passes in the duplex apartment of the Cavendishes, in the East Fifties, New York.

ACT I. *A Friday in November. Early Afternoon.*

ACT II. *Saturday. Between Matinee and Night.*

ACT III. *A Year Later.*

The following is a copy of the program of the first performance of the revival of "THE ROYAL FAMILY" as presented at the Helen Hayes Theatre, New York, N.Y., on December 30th, 1975:

Barry Brown, Burry Fredrik, Fritz Holt, Sally Sears

present

THE ROYAL FAMILY

a Comedy by

George S. Kaufman and Edna Ferber

Directed by Ellis Rabb

THE CAST

(In order of appearance)

DELLA .... *Rosetta Le Noire*
JO .... *John Remme*
HALLBOY .... *James C. Burge*
McDERMOTT .... *Sherman Lloyd*
HERBERT DEAN .... *Joseph Maher*
KITTY DEAN .... *Mary Louise Wilson*
GWEN .... *Mary Layne*
PERRY STEWART .... *Forrest Buckman*
FANNY CAVENDISH .... *Eva Le Gallienne*
OSCAR WOLFE .... *Sam Levene*
JULIE CAVENDISH .... *Rosemary Harris*
ANTHONY CAVENDISH .... *George Grizzard*
CHAUFFEUR .... *Miller Lide*
GILBERT MARSHALL .... *Donald Barton*
ANOTHER HALLBOY .... *Mark Fleischman*
GUNGA .... *James C. Burge*
MISS PEAKE .... *Eleanor Phelps*

IMPORTANT NOTE: For this highly successful Tony Award-winning revival by Ellis Rabb, many cuts and changes were made. They are to be found at the end of this volume beginning on page 171 to 174. The Owners recommend most strongly that this updated version be used.

The Royal Family

SCENE: *The scene is the duplex apartment of the Cavendish family, in the East Fifties, New York. The room is spacious, high-ceilinged, has a balcony. Rear center of balcony is an alcove, from which two doors, right and left, lead into bedrooms. A door at left of balcony that leads to additional rooms. A staircase leads to this balcony from about left center. Leading off the main room there are three doors. One is the outer door, set at a right angle. Under the stairs, right, is the door leading into the rear of the apartment. Down left is a double door leading into the library. A large window down right.*

The room has about it nothing of the commonplace. At a glance one sees that it is lived in by an unusual family. It is rich, careless, crowded, comfortable. Almost cluttering it are deep cushioned chairs, little corner clusters of couch, table, lamp; photographs in silver frames are all about; magazines, cushions. A profusion of flowers. Tapestries and rich shawls hang over the balcony railing. A grand piano is partly under the balcony, slightly to the left. A colorful brocade is thrown over this, and a lamp stands on it, together with photographs, etc. All sorts of periods and styles have gone into the making of the room. Prominently placed is a portrait in oils of the late Aubrey Cavendish in his most celebrated role, all bristling mustachios, high stick, romantic cape, glittering orders, gold braid, silk and boots and swagger. A shadow light is over this picture.

Down stage at the extreme right there is a table. In front of window R. *is a bench—at the upper end of the bench and facing the audience is a large over-stuffed chair. Directly back of this chair against the back flat is a secretary and chair. A grand piano is directly center with the keyboard* R. *There is a piano bench. In front of piano is a large sofa. Left of the sofa a small table. Next an armchair. Above the doors left is a commode, a chair and a coffee table. Below the doors is a small table and a chair. There is a French telephone, stands on the piano. Another (the house telephone) is under the stairs. The time is about one o'clock of a November afternoon. The Cavendishes, a family of actors, are only now stirring for the day.*

AT RISE: *At the rise of the curtain the stage is briefly empty. Immediately* DELLA, *the maid, comes from one of the bedrooms off the balcony, a breakfast tray in her hands. She looks a capable person, in the thirties, and intelligent enough to cope with the often surprising situations that arise in the Cavendish household.*

She has some difficulty in manipulating both the tray and the door. Finally manages to close the door with her foot. Then she rests the tray on the balcony rail for a moment of readjustment before starting the length of the balcony to descend the stairs. As she starts down the stairs the telephone rings. JO, *the houseman, enters down right, also carrying a laden tray. He is wearing a white housecoat. He is a man of about forty-eight or fifty.*

DELLA, *downward bound, naturally is the one to answer it. She hastens on down, looks about and puts her tray on a "coffee" table left of stairs.*

(HOUSE Telephone.)

DELLA. Hello! *(The house phone off stage, right, rings.* JO *is at the top of the stairs, and looks about in indecision, then puts the tray on the top step and comes hurriedly down and off right under stairs to the house phone. In the meantime* DELLA *is speaking on the outside phone.)* Yes. . . . No, she's not up yet. . . . I say she's not up yet. Well, I don't know. About an hour, maybe.

(JO *is now at the house phone, off. His conversation can be heard running through the rest of* DELLA'S *talk.)*

JO. Hello. . . . You can sign for them. . . . All right, send him up and I'll sign for them. *(He hangs up.)*

DELLA. Who is it, please? . . . Mr. Who? . . . Oh, Mr. Wolfe! . . . Yes, Mr. Wolfe? *(A more personal tone)* You know how it is here when the phone starts. . . . Yes, certainly, Mr. Wolfe. I will. All right.

(JO, *having finished his telephone conversation, has crossed rapidly and is well up the stairs.)*

DELLA. Who was on the house phone?

JO. Nothing. Only some flowers.

DELLA. *(A glance around the flower-laden room)* Just what we need.

(TELEPHONE.)

(Reaches for tray. Again the telephone.)

DELLA. Hello!

(BUZZER.)

(The sound of the back door buzzer.)

DELLA. The back door, Jo! (JO *disappears into* JULIA'S *room.)* Hello! . . . Yes. . . . Who is it, please? . . . Oh. . . . Yes, she's up, but she can't come to the phone. . . . Yes, I'll take. . . . Dinner at Mrs. Sherwin's—— (JO *appears from* JULIE'S *room.)*

(BUZZER.)

DELLA. Will you wait a minute, please? . . . Jo, that was the back door. Katie'll never answer.

JO. *(Annoyed)* All right. *(Exits right—under stairs.)*

DELLA. *(Again at phone)* Now what was that again? . . . Dinner at Mrs. Sherwin's, four thirty-six Park Avenue, November 26th, at seven. . . . Seven! I'll tell her, but Miss Cavendish has got to be in the theatre before eight—she always eats dinner six-thirty. . . . Yes, I will. *(Hangs up.)*

(JO *enters from under stairs. In his arms stacked high and tied together are pasteboard boxes, very large ones at the bottom, and smaller ones at the top. These reach almost to* JO'S *chin.)*

JO. Where do you want these?

DELLA. Who they for? Miss Julie? Take 'em up to her room. (JO *goes toward stairs. A* HALLBOY *enters behind him, bundle laden. He pauses just a moment, peers around his stack of boxes to get his bearings.)* Right on up.

HALLBOY. There's more. *(Follows* JO *up.)*

(DELLA *exits right.* MCDERMOTT, *the trainer, enters on balcony from* JULIE'S *room, whistling. A dapper, slim, quick ferret with a left cauliflower ear and an amazing co-ordination of muscle. He reeks of the ring. He is wearing a white flannel sleeveless undershirt, trousers, a belt. Has on one boxing mitt, carries the other.)*

McDermott. *(Speaking as he enters)* All right, Miss Julie, I'll see if I can—— (McDermott, *on balcony, steps aside for* Jo, *who is at the top of the stairs. Surveys the laden two.)* Somebody moving in?

Jo. One side! Heads up!

McDermott. G'wan! (Della *enters from under stairs carrying additional boxes.)* Je's!

(DOOR Bell.)

(Jo *exits* Julie's *room.* Hallboy *still ascending stairs. The doorbell rings.* Della *has an instant of indecision. Puts down her boxes. Starts for door. Telephone rings.* Della *goes toward it. Changes her mind, continues to door. Telephone continues.* McDermott *comes down.* Jo *reappears on balcony. Comes down.)*

(TELEPHONE.)

Della. Jo, answer the telephone. *(Exits in hallway.)*

Jo. Let it ring!

McDermott. *(To* Della) Seen Miss Julie's mitts?

Della. In the library.

McDermott. Where?

(VOICE Off.)

Messenger. *(Voice off. Very loud)* Telegram for Cavendish.

Jo. *(Picking up* Della's *pile of boxes)* Only ring again if I do answer it. *(Starts for stairs.)*

McDermott. Where'd you say? (Della *down from door, with telegram in hand.)*

Della. In the library. Jo, you got a pencil?

(McDermott *exits into library, left.)*

Jo. *(Over the top of his boxes)* Have I got a pencil!

(Hallboy *out of* Julie's *room. Down stairs.)*

Della. Well, I can't answer—— Oh, for heaven's sake!

(Hallboy *exits.)*

(STOP Phone.)

Della. *(In phone)* Hello! . . . Miss Julie Cavendish? . . . Well, she can't just now.

McDermott. *(Enters from library, whistling)* I found 'em!

Della. Oh, I should think in about an hour.

McDermott. I bet Jo was using them.

(Jo *enters from* Julie's *room. Starts down. He carries a pair of women's shoes.)*

(BUZZER.)

Della. All right. I'll tell her. *(Hangs up. The back door buzzer sounds.)* What's that?

Jo. I guess it's those flowers.

Della. I'll go. Here, you take this up to her. *(Hands him telegram.)* Give me those. *(Takes shoes. Buzzer sounds again.)*

(BUZZER.)

(McDermott *has taken off his gloves, put on the other pair. Tucks original gloves under his arm.)*

DELLA. Oh, all right, all right! *(Exits right.)*

JO. *(Gets card tray from hallway, places telegram on it—then comes to piano)* How's the battler, huh? Pretty good?

MCDERMOTT. Say, I'm always in good condition. A little boxing wouldn't hurt you none. You got flat feet carrying trays.

JO. *(Lays tray on piano—picks up cigarette box)* Any fellow goes around boxing women for a living I guess I could take 'em on.

MCDERMOTT. Yeah! I've took on some of the best in the world in my time.

JO. *(Crosses left with cigarette box)* I know your record. You was known as Canvasback McDermott. You're right in your class now, all right. Running a gymnasium racket, hiring out as a punching bag for women to keep their figures. *(Has come* L. *to commode and filled the cigarette box.)*

MCDERMOTT. All right, and let me tell you something. I got some clients could make a jelly out of you, and what do you know about that!

JO. Yeah!

MCDERMOTT. Yeah. *(Points to stairs)* She give me a poke yesterday would have held you for the count.

JO. I'd like to see her try it. *(Crosses back to piano—puts down cigarette box—picks up tray and telegram.)*

MCDERMOTT. I trained a lot of stage people, but I never seen anybody pick it up quicker than Miss Cavendish.

(DOOR Bell.)

JO. I bet the old lady herself could take you on. Now, I been here upwards of ten years, and—— *(The outer door bell rings.* JO *starts toward it, still talking)* and nothing they could do—— *(Remembers telegram. Gives it to* MCDERMOTT.) Here. Take that, will you? You're going up to Miss Julie's room. (McDermott *is on his way up the stairs.)* Say, do you think you could get me into the Garden Friday night? I've never seen this Delaney.

McDermott. Sure. Just mention my name.

(Takes the last few steps in a great leap. Exits. Jo *opens outer door. The well-rounded tones of* Herbert Dean *are heard in greeting.)*

Dean. Ah, good morning, Jo, my boy! Good morning!

Jo. Good morning, Mr. Dean.

(Dean *strides into the room.* Jo *shuts outer door and follows.* Dean *is about fifty-seven, very dressy, an excellent actor, beginning to show his age. The flower of the Lambs' Club. Necktie, shirt and handkerchief always blend. Massage has been his most active form of exercise. His appearance inevitably brings to mind the adjective "well-preserved." Clothes a shade too well tailored. His topcoat is one of those which define the waistline. His walking stick is London. Under his arm is a play manuscript. His entrance is a characteristic one, done in state. That springy walk.)*

Dean. Well, well, well! Where's the family! Where's everybody! *(Drops script on sofa—gives* Jo *hat and stick.)*

Jo. They're not down, Mr. Dean. It's hardly half past one yet.

Dean. *(Removes coat)* I was up a full hour ago. Setting up exercises! Cold bath!

Jo. *(Taking coat)* Yessir! You always took care yourself. That's how you kept your figger.

Dean. *(Goes up right, looks in mirror)* Yes. Well, look here. They're all awake, aren't they?

Miss Julie's awake? *(Takes out cigarette-case—finds it empty—fills it from box on piano.)*

JO. *(Takes hat and coat in hall)* Oh, yes. Her and the trainer been exercising half an hour and more. She ought to be down any minute now.

DEAN. I see. I see. I want very much to talk to her before we're interrupted. *(Picks up his script.)* How about my sister? *(Goes left.)* She up? *(A glance to balcony bedroom door.)*

JO. *(Enters)* She's been stirring quite a while. Doesn't sleep so well lately. Mrs. Cavendish doesn't. Wide awake at nine thirty every morning.

DEAN. (DEAN *has noticed the breakfast tray and drifts toward it, talking as he walks, but intent on the tray)* Well, of course she's getting along in years. *(DOOR Bell. Two Long Peals.)*

(Door bell rings. He feels the coffee pot to learn if it's hot. Dreamily picks up a breakfast roll. Butters it.)

DEAN. Trouble is, she won't give in. Pretends she's well——

(Two long and determined peals of the door bell. An apprehensive look in DEAN'S *face. Munching the roll, he crosses down left.* JO *opens outer door to admit* KITTY LEMOYNE DEAN.)

JO. Good morning, Mrs. Dean! And how are you this morning?

KITTY. *(Off stage)* Is Mr. Dean here?

JO. Yes, he just got here! *(Off stage.* KITTY *enters. About forty-eight, but doesn't believe it. An actress for many years, never more than mediocre. She is obviously in a temper. She remains right. Stands regarding him with a baleful eye. They glare at each other.* DEAN *turns away with a snort.* JO *comes down, is in a genial mood and essays a pleasantry.)* That's funny. You getting here just a minute after Mr. Dean. He must got here a minute ago himself. *(He looks expectantly from one to the other, for appreciation of this coincidence. Something in their faces tells him that things are not so jolly.)* Well, I'll tell Miss Julie you're both down here. *(He retreats, somewhat gingerly—going to stairs.* DELLA *enters from under stairs breezily. She is carrying box of flowers tied with ribbon.)*

DELLA. Good morning, Mrs. Dean! Mr. Dean! You two are out bright and early!

JO. Psst! *(A bit of warning pantomime from* JO *to* DELLA. DELLA *gives to* JO *an uncomprehending look.)*

DELLA. H'm? (KITTY *barely glances at* DELLA. *A movement of the lips that is a frigid imitation of a smiling assent.)* Well, I'll tell Miss Julie you're here. (DELLA *exits upstairs.* JO *picks up tray that* DELLA *brought down earlier. Starts toward door, right.)*

DEAN. Yeh! Here, here! *(Snatches another roll from tray.)*

JO. Why, you're hungry, sir. Won't you let me bring you a bite of breakfast!

DEAN. No, no, no, no! . . . (JO *starts right.)* I'll tell you what. You might bring me a cup of coffee.

JO. *(Stops center)* Yessir! I'll have it made fresh for you.

DEAN. Thanks, Jo. I wasn't permitted to finish my breakfast this morning, what with one thing and another. *(With a meaning glare at* KITTY.)

JO. Yes, sir! *(A backward look around the edge of the upraised tray that inquires as to* KITTY'*s possible need of refreshment.)*

(READY Phone.)

JO. Perhaps—you—would—like—— (KITTY'S *stony look defeats him.* JO *exits under stairs.* KITTY *and* DEAN *are alone.* DEAN *takes a vicious and defensive bite of roll.)*

KITTY. And, furthermore, Herbert Dean, if you think you can shut me up by sneaking off to this family of yours——

DEAN. Sneaking, my good woman! I believe I am privileged to walk out of my own home and call on my niece and my sister without asking your formal permission.

KITTY. If you think I'm going to stand by and see another woman play that part—— *(Simultaneous)*

KITTY. You're mighty mistaken. That part was made for me! I'd be marvelous in it! And if you imagine for one minute, Herbert Dean——

DEAN. For heaven's sake, Kitty. I've been waiting ten years to get a play like this—but I tell you it isn't for you! It's——

(Both stop at the sound of a door opening on the balcony. They glance up. DELLA *appears.* DEAN *throws the manuscript back on the table with a slam and turns left.* DELLA *comes down. She has just exited right and* KITTY *has taken breath for a renewal of the attack when the phone rings.* DELLA *returns.* KITTY *sits on sofa.)*

(AS DELLA *Comes Down Stairs, Phone.)*

DELLA. *(At phone)* Hello! Yes. Mr. Anthony Cavendish? Oh, no, Mr. Anthony Cavendish is not here. . . . Yes, he lives here when he's home, but he's in *Hollywood*. . . . I don't believe he's expected. *(To* DEAN*)* Is Mr. Tony expected?

DEAN. I don't know.

DELLA. No, he isn't expected. . . . Who is it, please? . . . The Graphic?

DEAN. *(A warning whisper)* You don't know anything.

DELL. *(In phone)* I don't know anything. *(Hangs up.)*

DEAN. What did they want?

DELLA. Said Mr. Tony. I told them he was in Hollywood.

DEAN. The Graphic. What's that young devil up to now? *(Sits in chair left of* C.)

KITTY. A Cavendish can do no wrong.

DELLA. I told Miss Julie you wanted to see her in a hurry. (DELLA *exits right.)*

KITTY. In a hurry, h'm? Before I could get here!

DEAN. Now, Kitty, let's not go all over this again. Look at me! I'm all unstrung. I've had no sleep.

KITTY. You had as much sleep as I had.

DEAN. Whose fault was it! Let me tell you, madam, one more night like that and I move to the Lambs' Club.

KITTY. Move! Where do you think you live now!

DEAN. *(Rises, picks up script)* I won't have any more talk about it.

KITTY. No, I'm not allowed to say a word. But you sent a script over for Julie to read last night—Julie and that sister of yours.

DEAN. And why shouldn't they read it! I have never done a play without consulting Fanny and Julie.

KITTY. Maybe that's why you never have a hit.

DEAN. I'll have one this time! I can see myself in every line of it, every gesture! Take the Nero scene! *(A pose.)* And as Abraham Lincoln. But you, my dear Kitty—you are no longer—uh—h'm! You see, your technique is more—uh—mellow——

KITTY. Are you by any chance telling me I'm too old! *(Rise.)*

DEAN. Oh, my dear Kitty!

KITTY. Then I suppose I'm not good enough actress! I was good enough to support Mansfield, though, wasn't I!

DEAN. Plenty!

KITTY. I'm as good an actress as your precious Julie. And I'm better than that sister of yours ever was.

DEAN. My dear Kitty, please do not embarrass me by comparing yourself with Julie Cavendish, or with my sister, the greatest Lady Macbeth of her day.

KITTY. Cavendish! Cavendish! I'd had the royal family Cavendished up to me for twelve years. God, but I'm sick of them!

DEAN. *You* are sick of the Cavendishes! *You* are—— And who are you, I'd like to know, to be sick of the Cavendishes! What were you when I married you!

KITTY. I was understudying Mannering in "The Garden of Allah."

DEAN. You were an off-stage noise!

KITTY. I was doing——

(JO *enters, with* DEAN'S *tray. Slight pause on threshold to make certain battle is not too thick.)*

JO. Here you are, Mr. Dean. Nice hot pot of coffee pick you up right away. *(Puts tray on table, left of stairs.)*

DEAN. Thanks, Jo, thanks. Coffee! That's fine!

JO. Hot buttered toast. *(Lifts a napkin.* KITTY *sits on sofa.)*

KITTY. Oh, Jo! (JO *pauses.)* I feel a little faint. *(An eye on the tray.* DEAN *loops hopeful.)* Perhaps if I forced myself to swallow a mouthful of coffee——

JO. Right away, Mrs. Dean. And a little toast?

KITTY. The tiniest sliver. . . . Or perhaps I ought to try to eat an *egg*.

JO. I'd try, yes, ma'am. Soft boiled?

KITTY. I think—shirred. With just a thin curl of bacon.

JO. Thin curl of bacon. Yes'm. *(Turns to go.)*

DEAN. I—uh—h'm—I might have an egg, Jo, while you're about it.

(SLAM Door.)

JO. Yes, sir. Same as Mrs. Dean's? *(The sound of the outer door closing.)*

DEAN. Why—ah——

(GWEN *enters from outer door. She is in riding clothes; a slim lovely young thing of nineteen. She is, perhaps, less a* CAVENDISH *than any of the others of the family.* PERRY STEWART *enters behind her and lingers a moment uncertainly in the doorway.* PERRY STEWART *is a personable young fellow of about twenty-eight. Piping Rocking, Long Island bonds. He is wearing an overcoat. His driving gloves are rather indicative of the Minerva at the curb.)*

GWEN. M-m-m, Jo, I've got to have some lunch. (JO *exits.* DEAN *and* KITTY *say "Hello" to* GWEN. *To the* DEANS) Hello. . . . What some lunch, Perry?

DEAN. Lunch?

PERRY. Not a chance! If I'm going to dress and get back here I've got to blow.

GWEN. This is Perry Stewart. Oh, I guess you've met. My Uncle—and Aunt Kitty. (PERRY *steps forward and shakes hands with* KITTY.)

KITTY. Been riding?

GWEN. Mm. It was marvelous. Jo, what've you got to eat? . . .

PERRY. Look here, don't you waste a lot of time on lunch. *(Looks at wrist watch.)* I'll be back here at half past two, and you're going to be ready.

GWEN. Very well, m'lord.

PERRY. No fooling, Gwen. It's an hour's drive, and a guest of honor has to be on time.

GWEN. That sounds scarey.

PERRY. Well—you know—one thing mother's fussy about is people being on time.

GWEN. I'll be sitting on the curb.

PERRY. She thinks actresses are temperamental, or something. So let's show her. *(To* DEAN *and* KITTY) Goodbye.

(They say goodbye. PERRY *goes out.)*

GWEN. Goodbye, Perry! (GWEN *follows him in hallway.)*

(DEAN *and* KITTY *also say "Goodbye.")*

JO. *(Enters. To* DEAN) Did you say the same as Mrs. Dean's, sir? The eggs?

DEAN. Oh. Yes. A little bacon—chicken livers—anything.

JO. Yes, sir. *(Starts to exit.)*

GWEN. *(Enters from hallway)* What you got for me, Jo? Cold meat, or a chop—I don't care so long as it's food.

JO. Yes, Miss Gwen. (Jo *exits right.)*

GWEN. Gosh, I'm hungry! I was up at half past seven. *(Removes hat.)*

DEAN. Half past what!

KITTY. I think he's awfully good looking, Gwen.

GWEN. *(Coming down)* I'll tell him.

KITTY. What's the function this afternoon? It sounds formal.

GWEN. Oh, no. Perry's mother is giving a tea for me, that's all. *(Is going up the stairs.)*

DEAN. Uh—Gwen. You might remind your mother that I am waiting. And also your grandmother.

GWEN. Sure.

KITTY. Incidentally, so am I.

DEAN. No more morning rides after this week, eh, Gwen, my child? Rehearsals. Rehearsals.

GWEN. I'm afraid so.

DEAN. You ought to be very proud, my dear. At your age, to be appearing with your mother. Quite an event! Quite an event in the theatre! *(Toast and napkin in hand, he gives the effect of a speech as his mood gains in warmth and splendor)* Yes, sir! About to enter into your great inheritance? To come before the public as the descendant of a distinguished family! It is not a trust to be taken lightly, my dear. Remember that not only will all of us be watching you, but your gifted ancestors as well. *(A heavy "Ahem" here.)*

(GWEN *has lingered politely near the top of the stairs.* FANNY CAVENDISH'S *door opens and she enters quickly from the balcony. She speaks simultaneously with the opening of the door.)*

FANNY. I think that speech needs cutting, Bertie.

(FANNY CAVENDISH *is seventy-two. Managerial, pungent, rather magnificent. Given to domineering and to reminiscence. Her clothes are rich, but careless, and somewhat out-dated.)*

GWEN. How are you, baby? Feeling all right?

FANNY. Splendid. . . . Have a nice ride?

GWEN. Glorious! The sun over the frost——

FANNY. Spare me. (GWEN *exits door right on balcony.* FANNY *starts down stairs.)* Yes, Bertie, they'd be up the aisles and out before you'd really got your teeth in it. *(Is descending stairs)* Isn't that hat a little ingenue, Kitty? (DEAN *goes to meet* FANNY, *foot of stairs.)*

DEAN. How are you this morning, Fanny? What did the new doctor say? Anything?

FANNY. What do they know? Parcel of fools! . . . *(As* DEAN *tries to assist her. Descends the last step)* Well, what brings you two love birds around at the break of day?

KITTY. Your devoted brother is calling one of his family conclaves.

DEAN. I'm here to see Julie, that's all.

FANNY. *(Crossing to her chair)* Family conclave, eh? Sounds very repulsive.

DEAN. *(Following and trying to assist her)* Allow me.

FANNY. It's all right. Don't fuss, Bertie. I'm not helpless. *(Sits.)* Julia not down yet, eh?

DEAN. She is not. I've been waiting half an hour. *(Crosses left.)*

FANNY. That prize fighter's here, I guess. When I was Julie's age I didn't have to have prize fighters to keep my figger. You could span my waist with your two hands.

KITTY. I like a nice womanly figure myself.

FANNY. You ought to be very happy.

DEAN. Well, Fanny, you certainly don't seem an invalid. You're looking splendid. *(Crosses to his tray.)*

FANNY. Invalid? Well as I ever was. I am going into rehearsal as soon as Wolfe can pick a cast.

DEAN. Now, now, Fanny. You've had a long siege of it. After a year's illness—— *(Picks up his cup of coffee.)*

KITTY. Nearer two, isn't it?

FANNY. And what if it is! Two years out of a lifetime! I played fifty-three years without missing a performance, except when Tony was born.

KITTY. And surely when Julie was born!

FANNY. No, sir. She knew her business better than that. Julie was born during Holy Week.

DEAN. But look here, now, Fanny. What are you going to do? You haven't a new play, have you? *(Sits left* C., *sips coffee.)*

FANNY. Who said anything about a new play! I'm reviving "Mrs. Castlemaine."

DEAN. But that's rather old-fashioned, Fanny. New York won't come to see that, even with you in it.

FANNY. New York! You talk like a Follies girl! I'm going to take it on the road.

DEAN. The road? You're mad.

FANNY. I know your views, Bertie.

DEAN. I don't belittle the road. It's quite all right in its way. But my public is in New York.

KITTY. Or was, when last heard from.

FANNY. Well, I'm not like you, Bertie. I've been a trouper all my life, and I'm going to keep on trouping. I'd rather pack 'em into a tent in Texas than play highbrow matinees at the Teacup Theatre in New York.

DEAN. But you've been ill, Fanny. You can't stand what you used to. Those dreadful small town hotels! Sleeping in Pullmans——

FANNY. I did it when there weren't any Pullmans! When many a time I had to sit up all night —yes, with Julie asleep on one side, and Tony generally yelling his head off on the other.

DEAN. But that belongs to the past, Fanny. You're too important a figure today.

FANNY. *(In spite of her infirmity rises to her feet)* I was Fanny Cavendish then, just as I am now. When the bills said Aubrey and Fanny Cavendish people *knew* what they were *going to see.* You had to know how to act—*(A slow turn toward* KITTY*)*— when you went on the stage in those days.

KITTY. You had your method. We of the younger school have ours.

FANNY. Ah, youth, youth!

DEAN. *(Rise. In the manner of a formal announcement)* If you do go back this season, Fanny, that's going to mean the whole family on the boards. *(Returns his cup to tray.)*

FANNY. The whole family?

(DOOR Bell.)

DEAN. Except Tony, of course. You can't call pictures acting. . . . But with you in "Castlemaine," Julie and Gwen in their play, and—*(A triumphant reach for the manuscript on the table. The doorbell rings.)*—your humble servant as the star of——

FANNY. *(In a surprising shout—picks up daily paper from piano)* Della! Della! *(Turns to* DEAN *again)* What's that about your being the bright particular star?

DEAN. I sent the manuscript of my next play over to Julie last night.

FANNY. I know it. (KITTY *rises,* DELLA *enters right. Goes to outer door.)*

DEAN. Have you read it?

FANNY. Only the first four scenes. (JO *enters with* KITTY'S *tray.)*

DEAN. Well?

FANNY. I was afraid to read the second act for fear you played two parts at once. *(Sits in her chair* R.)

DELLA. *(At door)* Good morning, Mr. Wolfe.

WOLFE. *(Off)* Morning, my girl. Good morning.

JO. *(Speaks through others)* Here you are, Mrs. Dean. All nice and hot. *(Places tray at window right.)*

KITTY. Oh—food!

(The thought palpably repels her, though she begins to eat. JO *places tray on tray bench up right and brings it in front of armchair near window.* OSCAR WOLFE *enters, followed by* DELLA, *who waits.* WOLFE *is a figure of authority; dark,*

stocky, slightly gray, dressed with a picturesque richness. A rakish black velour hat. Altogether the entrepeneur.)

WOLFE. Well, well. Good morning, folks! Hello, Bert! *(Gives his coat, hat and stick to* DELLA.)

DEAN. Ah, Oscar! Just the man I want to see.

WOLFE. *(Shakes a chiding finger)* Calories, Kitty! Calories!

KITTY. *(Her mouth full)* I didn't have a bite of breakfast.

WOLFE. Fanny, my girl, how are you! *(Takes her hand, pats it warmly.)*

FANNY. What brings you around this hour?

WOLFE. What draws me here always but the one great passion of my life! You, my dear Fanny!

FANNY. Now—now—what are you here for?

WOLFE. The heartlessness of this coquette! The best years of my life I've given her.

DEAN. Ah—Oscar—just——

WOLFE. *(Not heeding* DEAN. *To* FANNY) Where's your gifted daughter?

FANNY. I thought so. . . . Della, tell Miss Julie.

(GWEN *appears from center door, balcony.* DELLA *exits under stairs.)*

GWEN. My lunch ready? I'm dying. *(Wears silk riding shirt, breeches, mules and gay bathrobe.)*

JO. I'll bring it right in. *(Exits right.)*

WOLFE. Hello, there, young lady! How's the child actress! *(Meets* GWEN *at foot of stairs.)*

GWEN. Well, if it isn't Oscar himself! Here at the first pale crack of dawn!

WOLFE. Crack of dawn, huh? Say, you good-for-nothing actors can sleep till noon. You know your poor old manager's done a day's work for you already. That's quite a costume! What are you supposed to represent?

GWEN. (JO *enters with* GWEN'S *tray. He takes it left below door)* I'm the Spirit of Quick Lunch. . . . Bring it over here, Jo. Don't you want something, Mr. Wolfe? H'm? Haunch of venison or a couple of bear steaks?

FANNY. Jo! Time for my eggnog, isn't it?

JO. Yes, Mrs. Cavendish. They're beating it up.

WOLFE. *(A slow inclusive look around that takes in the three trays)* Don't you ever get mixed up, Jo, about who wants breakfast and who wants lunch?

JO. Yes, sir, certainly do, Mr. Wolfe. Still, you get used to it. (JO *transfers one dish to* DEAN'S *tray.)*

WOLFE. Say, do you people realize that there actually are families in this town that sit down in a dining-room all at the same time and eat a meal! Together!

FANNY. Quaint!

GWEN. I think it would be nice.

JO. Sure you wouldn't care for anything, Mr. Wolfe? Glad to get it for you.

WOLFE. No, not me, thanks, Jo. Lunch is a meal I never eat. (JO *exits at right.)*

FANNY. No. Just a little thick soup, and a mixed grill and coffee and French pastry at the Astor.

WOLFE. You're your old self this morning, Fanny. *(Crossing to* FANNY.)

FANNY. My old self, Wolfe, and ready to go back to work. *(A quick movement from* DEAN. *He wants to speak of himself.)*

WOLFE. Now, now, Fanny! Not so fast!

FANNY. Don't you now-now-Fanny me! I know whether I'm well or not. You haven't time for anything nowadays but Julie and Gwen productions.

DEAN. *(Manuscript in hand, taps* WOLFE *on the shoulder)* Oscar, I tried to reach you all day yesterday——

WOLFE. Yesterday? A crazy day. This is the

last theatre I'll ever build. Contractors—*(crosses* C.) —plasterers, license commissioners! Where the devil is Julie? She can't stay in bed *all* day. (Jo *enters with eggnog, places it on* FANNY'S *table—then exits.* WOLFE, *at foot of stairs)* Julie!

FANNY. Julie! *(A shout that tops* WOLFE'S.)

JULIE. *(A voice from behind the bedroom door, balcony)* I'm busy.

FANNY. Wolfe is here!

JULIE. Give him my love!

WOLFE. I'm in a hurry!

(Nothing from the upper regions. A moment's expectant pause. WOLFE *turns away with an impatient shrug.)*

DEAN. Well, Oscar—I have finally found the play!

WOLFE. All right, all right. Later on. You're a fine actor, Bert, but remember that last opus you handed me. Well, well! *(Cross to* FANNY*)* What you got there, Fanny? Something good?

FANNY. Eggnog. I'm being built up.

WOLFE. Got a little schnapps in it, huh?

FANNY. Milk and eggs.

WOLFE. Say, to do you good it's got to have something in it. Let me send you a few bottles sherry to-morrow. I got some fine Amontillado over at the office.

FANNY. That'll help.

DEAN. Now, Wolfe. *(Slips the manuscript under* WOLFE'S *arm)* There's the script.

(DELLA, *who has gone up on balcony by back stairs, now enters from* JULIE'S *room, a great pile of garments in her arms, so stacked that she scarcely can see over them. Down the stairs, exits right.)*

WOLFE. All right. *(Up toward the piano. Tosses manuscript on piano)* I'll keep it in mind. *(Strikes note or two, idly.)*

DEAN. What a play! Richness, characterization, verisimilitude!

WOLFE. M-m-m-m! I read it anyhow. *(A bar or two of music)* That other piano as bad as this?

DEAN. I'll drop in on you first thing in the morning. Hear what you think. *(He goes back to his tray, right.)*

(WOLFE, *becoming more interested in the music, runs another bar or two. Then he sits and concentrates a bit more on a few notes, preparatory to playing the thing he has in mind.)*

FANNY. What's the name of it again, Bertie? This masterpiece.

DEAN. "The Conqueror." *(Another brief run on the piano from* WOLFE.)

FANNY. Are you going to do it soon?

DEAN. Oh, around the holidays, if that suits Oscar?

(A glance toward WOLFE. WOLFE *is now playing, lightly, a melodious, slightly sentimental air that continues for a few bars without interruption.)*

GWEN. *(Goes to piano, gets cigarette, goes back to her tray. During a moment's lull in the music)* What's that?

WOLFE. I don't know.

(For a moment they give an ear to the music. JO *comes down to* FANNY *with a plate of rolls.* FANNY *refuses it. While the music is still playing,* JO *crosses to* KITTY, *offers her the rolls.*

They have all resumed eating. Their attention is fixed on the food before them. A brief lull. The music softly continues. The tinkle of silverware and the clatter of china is distinctly heard. The door of JULIE'S *bedroom opens slowly.* JULIE *appears, balcony.* JULIE CAVENDISH *is thirty-nine, beautiful, slim, mature. She is wearing a smart, rather tailored afternoon gown. Is evidently dressed for the day. She comes out slowly, curious to know who is playing. She crosses the width of the balcony, stands at the railing, looking down. Her first glance is toward the piano. She sees* WOLFE *there. Her gaze encompasses the rest of the room. Four of its occupants are busily eating. One at a time, she takes them in.)*

JULIE. Have you a table for one, Jo, not too near the music? (WOLFE *stops playing. Turns quickly to look up at* JULIE. DEAN *also looks up at her; and* KITTY.)

WOLFE. How do you ever make it on matinee days, Julie?

JULIE. *(Starts toward stairway)* By being the star, Oscar. They wait for me. *(She is leaning over the stairway rail, one hand posed just a little too carefully on the bannister.)*

FANNY. A very good entrance, Julie.

JULIE. Dear little mother! Wouldn't you like to go up and come down again? *(Comes on down.* GWEN *rises from her table, a bit of food in her hand, munching as she goes. She meets* JULIE *at the foot of the stairway)* Have a nice ride, Gwen? *(A glance at her)* Don't you look terrible!

(DELLA *enters, right, carrying a gay orange and purple figured box.)*

GWEN. I know it, mother. I'm going right up and change.

JULIE. No. Wait a minute. *(Flicks open the telegram in her hand and holds it out)* For lo, I bring tidings! Guess what!

FANNY. Tidings?

GWEN. Well?

DEAN. What?

DELLA. *(Indicates hat box)* A C. O. D. package, Miss Julie. Thirty-nine dollars.

JULIE. What?

DELLA. Thirty-nine dollars. A package.

JULIE. Thirty-nine dol—— What did I buy for thir—— Such a strange sum. Who has thirty-nine dollars? *(Surveys the group rapidly)* Oscar! Let me have it, will you? That makes—how much do I owe you now?

WOLFE. Enough. (MCDERMOTT *appears from center door, balcony. He wears coat, small black derby; little black bag in his hand. Starts down.)*

GWEN. Mother, I can't wait. You haven't any news, anyhow.

JULIE. Oh, but I have, Gwen, so come right back here. *(Glimpses* MCDERMOTT *coming swiftly down the stairs)* I'll want you to-morrow, you know, Mac.

MCDERMOTT. *(Shifts his hat slightly by way of deference)* Yes, Miss Cavendish, we'll have a real workout to-morrow. Same time? *(Crossing* R.)

JULIE. No, come at eleven—No—Bendel! Ten? . . . Oh, my God, no! . . . Twelve . . . one . . . one, Mac.

FANNY. Matinee tomorrow.

JULIE. Oh, good Lord, I can't make it tomorrow at all, Mac. . . . Monday.

WOLFE. Watch out there! You got rehearsals starting Monday.

JULIE. Wait a minute, Mac. So I have. Let me think . . . could you give me Sunday?

MCDERMOTT. I don't generally work Sundays as a rule. But, seeing it's you. One o'clock.

JULIE. One's fine. You're a dear.

MCDERMOTT. So long. (MCDERMOTT *starts to go.)*

JULIE. Good Lord! Mac! I can't Sunday! Make it to-morrow at twelve! I'll get it in some way.

MCDERMOTT. Yes, ma'am. *(Exit.)*

(DELLA *exits with package.* JO *on and off with* GWEN'S *tray.* JULIE *picks up her photographs from secretary—looks them over.)*

JULIE. Special fitting on Sunday, and it may take hours. Oscar, her second-act dress is going to be lovely. And, of course, the sable wrap will make it perfect.

WOLFE. Sable wrap?

JULIE. Why, of course. For the opera scene. She has to have a sable wrap.

FANNY. Wouldn't surprise me if the whole cast wore 'em. My day it was Fanny Cavendish's costumes by Fanny Cavendish. With one little dress and a guipure lace flounce I could be anything from Camille to the Two Orphans.

JULIE. I've seen that one little dress in the storehouse. The investment for whalebone and buckram alone would have kept me in sables a lifetime. *(Goes left* C.)

GWEN. Mother, are you going to read that telegram or aren't you?

WOLFE. First, let me tell you what I came about. Then I get right out. *(A sigh of impatience from* GWEN.)

JULIE. No, no! You've got to hear this. We need you.

GWEN. Well, then, come on with it!

FANNY. Yes, Julie, I think you've built up a good suspense.

JULIE. *(Surveys her position)* Am I centre? . . . It's dear little brother Tony again.

FANNY. Tony!

DEAN. I knew it.

WOLFE. What's he done now, that bum?

KITTY. Plenty, is my guess.

JULIE. Well, his telegram is rather sketchy, but as nearly as I can make out, I gather that he's killed somebody.

FANNY. Anyone we know?

JULIE. *(Reads)* "Pay no attention to possible accounts of Deming incident injuries not fatal takes more than that to kill a lousy movie director I arrive New York Saturday California police have no authority outside state on no condition talk to reporters Zeta Kaydak on this train but no trouble so far as am locked in drawing room love to all of you he was dirty hound anyhow, Tony." Good old Tony.

KITTY. What did I tell you! *(Rises.)*

JULIE. It lacks a certain clarity, doesn't it?

FANNY. California police!

DEAN. What's this, what's this! *(There now ensues a babel of sounds—exclamations, conjectures, questions spoken together.)*

FANNY. What's it mean?

KITTY. You know Tony!

GWEN. What's it all about?

DEAN. Who's this Zeta Kaydak?

WOLFE. *(Comes over to* JULIE*)* Now, now—now! Just a minute. Let's get at this. This may not be so funny. *(Takes telegram.)*

FANNY. Do you think it's serious?

JULIE. Of course not, Mother. It never is.

WOLFE. *(Re-reading fragments of the telegram*

to himself, but aloud) Possible accounts of Deming incident——

GWEN. Deming is his director.

WOLFE. Arrive New York Saturday.

DEAN. That's to-morrow.

WOLFE. . . . Zeta Kaydak on this train . . .

KITTY. She's that Polish hussy.

(JO *enters, gets eggnog glass and* KITTY'S *tray—exits.)*

WOLFE. A fine business.

FANNY. What's she on the train for?

WOLFE. On no condition talk to reporters. . . .

JULIE. Reporters? Have there been any reporters?

DEAN. Before you were down. The Graphic.

JULIE. The Graphic. Whatever we've done, we've always kept out of the tabloids. *(Sits on sofa.)*

WOLFE. Yes, and who's kept you out, I'd like to know? *Wolfe!*

JULIE. Here's another chance for you. What are we going to do?

WOLFE. Now, wait a minute. Let's look this over. Maybe it's not as bad as it seems.

FANNY. No.

GWEN. Of course not, Grandma. Such a fuss because Tony's punched some director. I'm sure to be late. *(On her way up the stairs.* GWEN *exits center door, balcony.)*

WOLFE. *(Still concentrating on the telegram)* Now, the way I figure it, it was like this. The fella says something Tony doesn't like. Tony knocks him down, of course. And to keep from having to answer a lot of questions about it, he gets on this train.

JULIE. With the picture half finished, naturally.

WOLFE. Omaha he sent this from. Omaha last night. That means he got to Chicago this morning. Naturally he got on the Century. To-morrow morning you'll be just one happy family.

JULIE. Now we've got to keep the newspapers off him. They've been laying for him ever since that Mauretania thing.

KITTY. I must say I don't blame them.

DEAN. Yes, he never should have thrown that reporter overboard.

WOLFE. A big mistake.

JULIE. They're sure to know he's on the Century. They'll swarm on him at the station. He'll start to smash cameras. *(A gesture that says "Whoop!")*

FANNY. That poor boy

WOLFE. *(Snaps his fingers)* I tell you how I fix it. He don't come into Grand Central. He gets off at 125th Street.

JULIE. It doesn't stop there.

WOLFE. To-morrow it will—for one second. *(Points wisely to himself)* I get him off the train, I bring him here before the newspapers know it, he stays quiet a couple of weeks. If they find it out, he's having a nervous collapse—and nobody can see him.

JULIE. *(Rise)* Oh, Oscar! That'll be wonderful! There you are, Mrs. C. Everything grand.

FANNY. Everything grand! Who's this Zany woman? What's she doing on the train?

JULIE. Well—uh—Oscar, tell mother the facts of life. *(Crosses to stairs.)*

WOLFE. *(Pats* FANNY'S *shoulder)* Satisfied, Fanny? Huh? Your boy ain't in danger? *(*KITTY *crosses and sits on bench* R.*)*

FANNY. You're the manager.

WOLFE. Good! Now! If nobody else has got anything to do, that you would like to have me wait until you do it—Julie, you don't want to take a massage first, or something? . . . No? . . . Well, then, do you mind if I waste just a minute of your time on my business?

DEAN. *(Rise)* That's what I say! After all, we——

WOLFE. No, no, no, no! This is Julie. Julie, my girl, it is now—— *(His watch)* My God! Five minutes after two! I want you down town in my office--you and Gwen—three o'clock, sharp.

JULIE. Down town! What for? *(Protesting.)*

WOLFE. Now, don't start to holler before I tell you. I'm not so stuck on it, either, but we've all got to do it.

JULIE. Do what?

WOLFE. Who do you think came in on the Mauretania last night? Out of a blue sky—St. John Throckmorton.

JULIE. Oh! Is that all? *(Turns upstage—picks up magazine from commode left—then sits.)*

KITTY. Who's he?

WOLFE. Who's he? Only the fellow that wrote Julie's new play, that's all.

DEAN. Oh, the author!

JULIE. Send him *back.*

KITTY. I'd love to meet him.

WOLFE. Now, now, hold on a minute. We got to be nice to this fellow. He's given you a beautiful play here, and the point is he's going to write more of them. Now, you do that for me, huh, Julie? Be there with Gwen at three?

FANNY. The less you have to do with authors the better.

WOLFE. *(To* FANNY*)* That's right! Make it harder! *(To* JULIE*)* We call it settled, huh? You'll be there? Remember this fella's come all the way over from England.

JULIE. But an English author! If he landed

last night, won't he be lecturing this afternoon? *(They all laugh.)*

WOLFE. If you comedians will keep still a minute, I'll tell you what it is. This Throckmorton is a new playwright, and English to boot, and nothing will satisfy him he wants to read his play to the entire company. *(A shout of derision from them all.)* Now hold on a minute. This is a serious fellow—monocle, spats, gardenia—everything. With him this is part of being a playwright, reading the play aloud. The chances are he saw one of those photographs in the Green Room of His Majesty's Theatre, the whole company grouped around,—Sir Beerbohm Tree in the middle—and What's-his-name reading "The Gay Lord Quex" to 'em. *You* should try to talk him out of it. I spent the morning.

JULIE. I never heard anything so idiotic in my life! *(Rises)* It's fantastic! But if you're really serious, and you want me to do this, I'll sit through it—only it can't be this afternoon.

WOLFE. It's got to be this afternoon.

JULIE. Oh, no! *(Comes down)* Then the whole thing's off. It would take hours. I have an appointment.

WOLFE. Julie, how often do I ask a favor? Now, this fella has got another play that I'm crazy to get hold of. If we're all just a little bit nice to him—jolly him along—tell him how good he is. What do you say?

FANNY. To hell with him!

JULIE. But Oscar, why in the name of heaven does it have to be just this afternoon! Can't it be some other time?

WOLFE. Say, what's going on this afternoon? You going to be married?

JULIE. *(A startled look)* I can't, that's all, Oscar. I—can't! It's got to be some other time.

WOLFE. To-morrow you got a matinee. Monday you begin rehearsals.

JULIE. Well—Sunday.

WOLFE. Sunday he's out at Otto Kahn's. I tell you there is no other time for it. If you knew what you mean to him! He's all impressed about having you and Gwen in his first play. He knows all about you. Everything you've been in—all of you.

DEAN. Really!

KITTY. You don't say!

WOLFE. So you wouldn't even do this for your old manager, huh? You got some little appointment—tea, or to buy a hat—and compared to that Oscar don't matter.

JULIE. Oh, now, Oscar——

WOLFE. Well—never mind. The next time you ask me to do something for you—*(Turns* R.*)*—I do it anyhow.

FANNY. I don't believe in humoring playwrights, but if it's such a favor to Oscar, that's different . . . *(Then turns directly to* JULIE*)* What're you doing that's so important this afternoon?

JULIE. Well, I——

KITTY. I'd do it, busy as I am. *(Cross to piano.)*

FANNY. Pay no attention to her, Oscar—I'll see that she's there.

JULIE. Mother, you don't understand.

FANNY. Oscar's done a lot of things for you.

JULIE. You win, Oscar. At three o'clock—Enter Julie Cavendish, laughing.

WOLFE. That's my girl! *(Starts briskly toward outer door, buttoning coat with the air of one who has accomplished something. He talks as he is in hallway)* Now don't forget. Three o'clock at my office.

DEAN. Oscar, you're not going? *(Crossing—grabs up play and stands* R.*)*

(JO *enters, crosses left, gets* DEAN'S *tray.* WOLFE *enters from hallway, putting on hat and coat. Takes out his watch again, his coat half on.)*

WOLFE. It's now two-twenty. You and Gwen leave here quarter to three, sharp. *(Comes down again, stands near* JULIE*)* All right? I can depend on it?

JULIE. I'll be there. *(Stands near stairs.)*

WOLFE. That's the way to talk. Good-bye, everybody! *(Starts upstage toward outer door.)*

DEAN. *(Eager for a few last words to* WOLFE *about his play)* Heh! Oscar!

WOLFE. *(A little bewildered, glancing at the manuscript)* What's this?

DEAN. *(Highly offended)* Well, on my word! That is the play that——

WOLFE. Oh, yes, yes, yes, yes—— *(Into the alcove up.* DEAN *follows him rapidly.* KITTY *has been easing over toward* WOLFE *at the first sign of his departure. She now comes swiftly to the alcove, bent on pressing her own claim.)*

DEAN. Now, as I told you, there's a scene or two where I could use a better entrance.

WOLFE. Sure, sure! I read it to-night. Give you a ring in the morning. Excuse me if I run. *(To elevator)* Down! *(Exits.)*

(DOOR Slam.)

(Exits. The slam of the door. JO *exits with* DEAN'S *tray.)*

DEAN. *(Talking through* WOLFE'S *speech, continuing from his own last speech)* But that's a simple matter. The main thing is to get an absolutely—— Kitty, for God's sake! (DEAN *enters and goes left.)*

KITTY. *(Starts speaking cue—when* DEAN *says "A scene or two")* You are going to remember about me, aren't you? I've played nearly all those parts and there isn't one—— *(At the slam of the door both* DEAN *and* KITTY *break off.* DEAN, *at the slam of the door at* WOLFE'S *exit, strides on and across to left, hands in pockets, very disgruntled.* KITTY *follows him, bristling)* I'm on to you all right. You're afraid I'll give too good a performance. You won't surround yourself with anything but second-rate people—you don't want anybody that's really good. Let me tell you I don't purpose to be held down artistically just because I'm married to Herbert Dean. I'm important, too, don't forget. Ask any producer in New York——

DEAN. *(Cuts in about at "You're afraid I'll give too good a performance")* Good God, Kitty, I've been a star for years! It's simply that you're not suited to this play, that's all. It's entirely the wrong kind of part for you. I should think you'd want to help instead of hindering. You know very well you drive me crazy by your infernal——

JULIE. *(Cutting in on the double conversation. Cue—*KITTY*—"That's really good")* Oh, stop it, you two, will you! Stop it or get out of here! Go on in there and argue. I've been a star, you've been a star—I can't stand it, I tell you. Get out! Get out! Get out! *(Takes an arm of each and, while they are still arguing, propels them rapidly into the library, left. Slams the door on them. Turns swiftly her back to the door, slumps a little against it, exhausted. A deep breath. Leans against door. The telephone rings on stage.* JULIE'S *sigh breaks off in the middle)* Oh! *(A mock nod of deference in the direction of the phone.)*

(TELEPHONE Business.)

FANNY. Let it ring.

JULIE. Oh, you never can tell. *(Picks up the receiver)* Yes! . . . This is Julie Cavendish. . . . Yes, this is Miss Cavendish speaking. . . . Yes? . . . Yes. . . . *(To* FANNY, *picks up cigarette—looks for match)* You were right. . . . Well, I'll tell you, it's very difficult for me to take part in any benefit performances just at present. . . . December third. . . . Well, you see, I'll be playing and rehearsing at the same time. I'm afraid . . . Yes, I'm sure it's a very good cause. . . . The Newark Newsboys . . . The little . . . Oh, yes . . . Well, I will if I possibly can. *(One of those mirthless laughs in response to a bit of fulsome praise. Goes left—sits—gets match)* That's very kind of you. I'm so glad you enjoyed it. . . . No, I won't forget. . . . Century Theatre, December third. *(Hangs up. To* FANNY*)* Mother, will you remind me? Bronchitis on December third.

FANNY. I shall do no such thing! If you promised to play that benefit you'll play it—bronchitis or double pneumonia.

JULIE. The honor of the family! *(Sits on sofa.)*

FANNY. Now, Julie Cavendish, what's all this mooning about? What was this big renunciation scene? "I can't this afternoon. I can't . . ." *(A gesture.)*

JULIE. Gilbert's back.

FANNY. Gilbert?

JULIE. Gil Marshall. He's in New York. I had a note from him; and some flowers.

FANNY. So that's it. *(Rises* L.*)*

JULIE. You see, it would have been nice to have had the afternoon clear.

FANNY. Was he going to come here?

JULIE. He's calling up at four to find out. Della will have to explain to him, that's all. A play reading! I'd better not tell him that.

FANNY. So! *(Sits on sofa)* He's come back to New York to spend his millions, h'm? What's that they call him?—South American Diamond King?

JULIE. Emerald, mother. Much nicer.

FANNY. Emeralds or diamonds. When I think that if it hadn't been for me you'd have gone off to South America—given up your career—everything.

JULIE. I wonder what he's like now. He may have grown very charming. South America, and millions, and perhaps a little gray here. *(Touches her temple)* Sounds rather romantic.

FANNY. No more romantic now than he was nineteen years ago! Ah! What a siege that was!

JULIE. And what a demon you were!

FANNY. I had to be. You thought because he looked serious and didn't say much that he was doing a lot of deep thinking. I knew it was because he couldn't think of anything to say.

JULIE. You certainly acted like a mother in a melodrama.

FANNY. I told him, I said, "Here's a girl that's going to have fame and fortune—the world spread before her. Do you think that you can make up to her for all the things you'd rob her of!"

JULIE. Yes, yes, I know, mother. He went away, and we both lived happy ever after.

FANNY. How I ever got you where you are today is more than I know. You were always at the point of running off with some young squirt.

JULIE. But I never did. So it couldn't have been so serious.

FANNY. Serious enough for them! That young Earl of Pembroke who went off to Africa, and that Boston fellow that shot himself——

JULIE. He was cleaning his gun.

FANNY. They were always cleaning their guns. And when you finally married Rex Talbot!

JULIE. Mother, out of the whole crowd of them, why did I marry Rex?

FANNY. He was the weakest, I guess.

JULIE. I always said I wouldn't marry an actor. And Rex wasn't even a good actor. What was there about him, mother?

FANNY. Rex Talbot was a brilliant young loafer! And he had the most beautiful manners. He was the kind of man who could kiss your hand without looking silly.

JULIE. I guess that was what he was always doing when I needed him. That's one thing you will admit about Gil, Mother. He would have been dependable.

FANNY. When you're eighteen you don't marry a man because he's dependable.

JULIE. But when you're a little older, you begin to think that maybe——

FANNY. What's that?

JULIE. Don't be alarmed. But I am curious to see him again. I had it all staged so beautifully, too. I was going to wear my rose beige, and a hat with a brim, and be dignified and wistful, yet girlish withal.

FANNY. You can put on that act for him just as well after the show to-night. It's been nineteen years. What's a couple of hours more!

JULIE. No. Midnight isn't as kind to me as it used to be. I'm just vain enough to want to look my best.

FANNY. You are, eh?

JULIE. I want to look fresh and young and radiant.

FANNY. Is that all?

(GWEN *enters from the center door on the balcony. She is smartly dressed in an afternoon frock, and on her arm she carries her coat. Her hat is in her hand. She is singing blithely and carelessly the newest jazz song hit. She comes quickly down the stairs.)*

GWEN. *(At the foot of the stairs)* Has anybody seen my tan bag? *(Throws coat and hat on nearby chair.)*

JULIE. *(Remembering the engagement with* WOLFE*)* Gwen, you're not going out?

GWEN. *(Crosses left, looking about, then goes on swiftly down left to the library door)* I left it down here somewhere last night when—— *(Opens the library door.* DEAN'S *voice and* KITTY'S *are heard in conflict.* DEAN'S *rising clearly above* KITTY'S.*)*

DEAN. *(Offstage)* —over my dead body——

KITTY. *(Offstage)* —a woman like Fanny Ward—— (GWEN *bangs the door shut with a bewildered and startled expression.)*

FANNY. *(Half to herself)* Shouts and murmurs off.

GWEN. But I think it's in there.

JULIE. Gwen, was it this afternoon that you were going out to Westchester with Perry?

GWEN. Of course. He'll be along any minute. *(Coming left center.)*

JULIE. Gwen, you've just got to leave word for him, that's all. You can't go.

GWEN. Why not? What's the matter?

JULIE. We've got to go right down to Oscar's office. I promised.

GWEN. But, mother——

JULIE. I know. I just forgot you were going with Perry. It's all a reading of the play by Throckmorton. He got in last night. He's set on it. Wolfe made an awful fuss about it—a favor to him—we——

GWEN. Mother, that's absurd. You know I've had this date with Perry for a week. I've never met his mother. She's giving this tea just for me. It's the first time she's asked me. She's having all these people in. How can I—— (FANNY *rises, goes to her chair* R.)

JULIE. You can do it as well as I can, Gwen. I'm only doing it for Oscar.

GWEN. But it can be some other time.

JULIE. No—it can't. I've been all over it, and there isn't any other time. It's got to be this afternoon.

GWEN. *(Stamping childishly away from them)* Oh, for the Lord's sake!

FANNY. He picked a good day for it, this Mr. Thingambob.

GWEN. Why do *I* have to be there! I've read his old play!

JULIE. So have I, for that matter.

GWEN. *(On the verge of tears)* Why didn't you tell me sooner? You knew I had this date——

JULIE. I'm sorry, Gwen, but I gave up something just as important—and more so. If you think it's going to be any fun for me to sit there and hear a play read——

GWEN. *(Starts speaking cue "And more so")* —I wouldn't *care* if it wasn't Perry's mother, but she'll probably never ask me again. And I couldn't go if she did ask me. I'll be rehearsing all the time, and then, I'll be acting, and it'll just go on like that forever. First thing you know I'll be an old woman— *(Two long rings at the doorbell, followed by a terrific hammering at the outer door. The clamor is enough to stop them, mid-speech.)*

(DOORBELL.)
(POUNDING.)

JULIE. *(Startled)* What's that! . . . Jo! . . . Della! *(Goes up to alcove.)*

GWEN. What is it! *(Runs up to alcove.)*

(FANNY *pounds rapidly on the floor with her stick.* JO *appears swiftly, right, followed by* DELLA. *Both go to alcove,* JO *on a half run,* DELLA *walking very quickly. At the same time the double doors of the library are thrown open as* DEAN *and* KITTY *emerge, brought out by the unusual noise.)*

DEAN. What's the matter? What's going on?
KITTY. My, what a racket!

(With the others they go up toward outer door. They are huddled in a group as JO *opens the door. From offstage you hear their voices in surprise and alarm.* GRANDMA *alone is on stage.)*

JULIE. *(Off)* Tony!
GWEN. *(Off)* Tony!
FANNY. *(In a tone of unbelief)* Tony?
DEAN. *(Over his shoulder, to* FANNY*)* It's Anthony! *(At this point the group at the door break into a confused chorus of surprise, unbelief, amazement, interrogation, "But how did you get here!" "You were in Chicago this morning!" "We just got your telegram!" "What does this mean!" "I don't understand how you——" "Well, this is a surprise, Mr. Tony!"* (JO) *"Well, of all people!"* (DELLA) TONY'S *"Sh-shs-shs-sh!" attempting to silence them, sounds through this babel.)*

(TONY *enters, dramatically, elaborately, stealthily, his look and gesture cautioning silence. He is wearing an all-enveloping fur coat, the collar of which is turned up so that his face is concealed.*

The brim of his soft felt hat is pulled over his eyes. He comes down swiftly, almost in the manner of one who is backing away from something he fears. His face is turned away so that he is looking over his shoulder. His left coat sleeve, scarcely seen by the audience, hangs empty.)

TONY. Sh-shs-sh! Sh-sh, I tell you!

FANNY. Tony! It's really you!!

(JULIE, GWEN, DEAN, KITTY *have followed a few feet behind him, bewilderment in their faces. They are still exclaiming.* JO, *laden with luggage, follows. A hallboy and a chauffeur, also carrying* TONY'S *belongings.* JO, *laden with baggage, enters last.* DELLA *enters, stands upstage. Distributed among these servants are a violin case, half a dozen bags and suitcases, very smart and glittering; an overcoat, a rug, golf sticks, hatbox, tennis racquet. The barrage of questioning opens up again with* JULIE, DEAN, *and* KITTY *in the lead, overlapping each other's speech.* GWEN, *after the first flurry of the entrance, remembers her own problems. And while she is interested in* TONY'S *explanation, etc., she is plainly disturbed about* PERRY STEWART.*)*

JULIE. But Tony, how did you get here? It isn't possible!

DEAN. My dear boy, this is rather bewildering!

KITTY. Well, you're a great one! Of all the surprises!

FANNY. If this is one of your jokes, Tony Cavendish——

TONY. Sh-sh! Be quiet, will you, everybody!

Shut up! *(Complete quiet then, for a brief moment)* Somebody go out there—*(Points to the entrance, right)* and lock the back door! (Jo *exits.)* Gwen! *(Indicating library)* Take a look out of that window! See if there's a man out there in a long overcoat! (Jo *enters.* GWEN *vanishes a second only through library doorway. Appears again immediately)* Take everything up to my room, Jo!

JO. This way, boys. (Jo *starts quickly up the stairs, laden with luggage, a glance over his shoulder to indicate that the hallboy and the chauffeur are to follow him with their share of the burden. They follow.)*

TONY. Julie, have you got some change? I want a lot of change. *(Turns toward his mother. Tilts up her chin, gaily. Kisses her)* How's America's sweetheart? Aren't you glad to see your baby boy?

JULIE. Tony, will you explain this trick entrance? How did you get here?

TONY. I'll tell you in a minute. First I want some money. *(Glances up toward chauffeur, hallboy,* Jo, *on stairway. To* CHAUFFEUR*)* Let me see. You get twenty dollars. *(Aside to others)* He brought me in from Mineola. . . . You get ten—— *(To the* HALLBOY*)* And ten apiece for those fellows downstairs. How many are there?

HALLBOY. Three, sir. Two, and the doorman.

TONY. All right. You take forty, and you get twenty . . . and now remember, you fellows, if any of those reporters ask you, you didn't see me, I never came in here. You don't know anything about me. Do you get that?

HALLBOY. Yes, sir.

CHAUFFEUR. I get you.

TONY. Julie, let them have the money, will you?

JULIE. Jo, you attend to it. My bag's on my dresser.

JO. I'll see to it.

(*At the end of his own last line* TONY *has started to throw off his fur coat, shrugging his left shoulder free and revealing his left arm in a silk sling. A little shriek from* FANNY.)

FANNY. Tony! Your arm!
JULIE. You're hurt!
DEAN. Is it a serious injury?
KITTY. (*At sight of the arm*) Oh!
GWEN. (*Half aloud*) Oh, Tony!
TONY. It doesn't amount to anything. I hit him too hard, that's all. (FANNY *makes a pitying sound between tongue and teeth.*)
JULIE. How did it start in the first place?
DEAN. Let's hear about it.

(DELLA *enters right and starts toward stairway.*)

TONY. Della, I'm starved. I haven't had a bite for twelve hours. Bring me everything you've got. (DELLA *turns and exits right.*) First I've got to have a hot bath. Come on upstairs, everybody, while I take a bath.

(*With* KITTY *and* DEAN *in the lead,* KITTY *having one foot on the stairway, they all go up toward the stairs.* FANNY *goes to* DELLA—*instructs her regarding* TONY'S *food.*)

JULIE. Tony, will you listen to me! How did you get here to-day? You were in Omaha yesterday!
TONY. I flew, of course. Came by aeroplane from Chicago.
DEAN. Aeroplane!
KITTY. Flew!
JULIE. Tony Cavendish!
TONY. I couldn't come on a train. They're watching the trains. I've got to lay low in this apart-

ment till I sail. (JO *is seen to cross to* JULIE'S *room and returns counting money.)*

FANNY. Sail?

JULIE. Sail where?

TONY. Europe, of course. To-morrow on the Aquitania . . . God, I hate pictures . . . I've got to have a bath. If you want to hear the rest of it, come on up!

(TONY *starts again for the stairway, and* KITTY *and* DEAN *mount quickly ahead of him.* KITTY *in the lead.* JULIE *follows just behind.* GWEN *remains on stage. As they ascend the stairs,* TONY, JULIE, DEAN *and* KITTY *are talking constantly and simultaneously.)*

DEAN. What happened out there, Tony? How did you get into this fight?

TONY. Oh, this alleged director—he had it coming to him ever since we started to shoot. He put his girl into the picture and when she got stuck on me he got sore. The blow off came when we were out on location. Doing a desert scene and Deming picked out the worst camel in the pack, and said to me: "You ride that one." I took one look at it and said: "The hell I will!" He said: "Who's directing the picture?" "You're directing the picture, but you're not directing me. I'm through with it, and you can take this to remember me by." *(Exits in* FANNY'S *room.* FANNY *starts towards stairs, when* TONY *says, "Like hell I will," nods approvingly.)*

JULIE. *(Cue when* DEAN *says "fellow in his place")* Unless you've killed him, Tony, I don't see why they're making all this fuss. And as for your going to Europe, I think it's the most ridiculous thing I've ever heard of. And you walked out in the middle of the picture, of course. They'll probably sue you for a million dollars, and you'll never get another picture job. *(Over balcony railing at* GWEN, *just exiting)* Get your things on, Gwen—I'll be right down.

KITTY. *(Cue: when* JULIE *says "Making all this fuss")* I've always heard things about those directors, though I must say I met David Wark Griffith and you couldn't ask for a more perfect gentleman. He said to me, "Miss Le Moyne," he said, "if you ever want to go into pictures, come right to me."

DEAN. *(Cue: when* TONY *says, "Remember me by")* Perfectly right to put the fellow in his place. Catch me letting any whipper-snapper tell me what to do. I'd show him!

(TONY *exits ahead of the rest.* DEAN *and* KITTY *follow, then* JULIE. FANNY *is last.)*

FANNY. Who's this train woman? This Zickery Zackery. *(Exits.)*

(GWEN'S *mood throughout this scene has been one of thoughtful depression. After the general exit she stands upstage for a moment. She drifts down toward the sofa, where her hat and coat have been thrown, and sits. Without glancing at it, she picks up her hat. The hallboy and the chauffeur appear on the balcony and descend the stairs quickly. The* HALLBOY *leads. He is counting a little sheaf of crisp bills. The* CHAUFFEUR *is just putting his bills into his pocket. They exit under stairs.* GWEN *merely glances at them, resumes her position. With a little spasmodic gesture that is almost despairing she crumples her hat in her hand, beating one hand softly with the crushed felt hat. A deep sigh. She sits staring ahead of her.* JO *follows the chauffeur onto balcony, descends the stairs. The doorbell rings. The sound electrifies* GWEN *into sudden action.)*

(DOORBELL. Perry.)

GWEN. I'll go, Jo. *(Exits outer door.)*

(JO *picks up* TONY'S *fur coat and hat. Exits under stairs.)*

PERRY. *(Off. With exaggerated elegance)* Why! Fancy meeting *you* here!

GWEN. *(Off)* Oh, shut up, Perry!

(DOOR Slam.)

(The sound of the door closing. GWEN *comes down immediately, followed by* PERRY. *He is speaking the next line as he comes.)*

PERRY. Come on, get your bonnet on. I'd like to stop at the Riding Club and look at that horse, wouldn't you? It'll only take a minute.

GWEN. Oh, Perry!

PERRY. What's the matter?

GWEN. I can't go.

PERRY. What do you mean—you can't go!

GWEN. They're going to read the play down at Wolfe's office.

PERRY. What?

GWEN. The author's going to read the play. And of course they had to pick this afternoon.

PERRY. What are you talking about?

GWEN. I can't go with you, Perry. I've got to go to Wolfe's office to hear the play read. There's no way out of it. I've got to do it. Isn't that damn!

PERRY. You're joking.

GWEN. But Perry. I'm not! I know it sounds silly——

PERRY. Silly! It's cuckoo! I never heard anything

so ridiculous in my life. You can't mean you're breaking this date just to go and hear somebody read a play. . . . What play?

GWEN. The play! The play that goes into rehearsal on Monday. That Mother and I are doing.

PERRY. Why, good God, you've read it a thousand times. You read it to me!

GWEN. But this is different. The author's going to read it.

PERRY. Well, let him—the silly ass! What do you care!

GWEN. *(A long breath)* Now, Perry, please try to understand this. It's part of my job, and it's important.

PERRY. Important to hear some idiot read a play that you've read again and again!

GWEN. But it's more than that—it's a ceremony! *(Sits on bench.)*

PERRY. Gwen, you know as well as I do that we planned this thing a week ago. Mother's no Victorian, but, listen, you can't do a thing like this. She wouldn't understand.

GWEN. Perry! I want horribly to go! I made an awful fuss. But what could I do?

PERRY. *(Crosses* R.C.*)* You know, Gwen, this isn't the first time you've done this to me.

GWEN. Perry, please don't be unreasonable.

PERRY. I don't think I was unreasonable about New Haven, when we were all set to go to the game——

GWEN. But I explained. *(Rise)* I told you. You said you understood. Wolfe suddenly phoned—I had to go down to see the chap he'd got as juvenile. If it was somebody I couldn't stand—— And Wednesday I had to be photographed with Mother.

PERRY. Yes, I know. I know.

GWEN. Don't look so stern. You know this is all just because of the new play.

PERRY. Yeh. But there'll always be a new play. *(Looks directly at her)* Won't there?

GWEN. I realize it's inconvenient sometimes. It is for me, too.

PERRY. But what are we going to do about it, Gwen?

GWEN. If I can't go—I can't. *(Turns away* R.)

PERRY. *(Follows her over)* I'm not talking about that. I mean us! Look here, Gwen. You're no blue-eyed babe. I haven't dropped down on one knee and said will-you-be-mine, but you know I'm absolutely crazy about you. Don't you?

GWEN. Uh-hm.

PERRY. But what are we heading for? That's what I'd like to know. How's it all going to work out?

GWEN. Why—I don't know. What is there to work out?

PERRY. After all, you marry the person that you'd rather be with than anyone else in the world. But where'll you be half the time? Rehearsing, or something. *(Turns* R.C.)

GWEN. Now, don't be fantastic! Rehearsals last three weeks.

PERRY. All right. And then what! You're at the theatre every night. Your work will just begin when mine is all over. You'll have dinner at six. I'll probably not even be home. By midnight you're all keyed up and ready to start out, but I've got to be at work in the morning.

GWEN. But those things adjust themselves. Lots of other people have got around it. *(Sits on bench.)*

PERRY. I'd do anything in the world for you, Gwen. I'd die for you! But I can't be one of those husbands. Hanging around dressing rooms! Side-stepping scenery. Calling up the costumer. What am I going to do every night. See the show?

GWEN. But you wouldn't want me to be one of

those wives, would you! Bridge and household and babies!

PERRY. Well, why not! What's the matter with that!

GWEN. *(Rise)* Because I can't do that sort of thing any more than you can do the other. I'm an actress, Perry. An actress!

PERRY. Oh, what does that mean! Suppose you turn out to be as good as your mother—or better! What is there to it when it's all over? Get your name up in electric lights, and a fuse blows out—and where are you!

GWEN. I won't let you belittle my work. It's just as important as yours. I suppose the world would go to pieces if you didn't sell a hundred shares of Consolidated Whatnot for ten cents more than somebody paid for it!

PERRY. You can't compare business with acting. *(Goes* R.C.*)*

GWEN. Is that so? I can give you the names of actors and actresses of three hundred years ago—dozens of them! Name me two Seventeenth Century stock brokers.

PERRY. All right, I'll give up my work. That'll be dandy! And trail along behind you carrying your Pekinese, huh? . . . Not me!

GWEN. It's not a Pekinese! Oh, Perry, what are we talking like this for! It's horrible. *(Goes to him.)* Forgive me! How could I talk like that to you!

PERRY. It's my fault. I didn't know what I was saying.

GWEN. Perry—dear! *(He takes her in his arms.)*

PERRY. Oh, what does anything matter!

GWEN. Weren't we a couple of idiots! We've never quarreled before.

PERRY. And we won't again. There isn't anything that matters to me except you. Business and acting. We must have been crazy!

GWEN. And you're all that matters to me.

PERRY. Gwen darling! *(They kiss again)* You're wonderful. Now, come on, honey. It's late. *(Gets hat.)*

GWEN. What?

PERRY. Why, you are coming with me, aren't you?

GWEN. Oh, Perry!

PERRY. Huh?

GWEN. You haven't heard a word I've said. *(Crosses and sits in chair* R.)

PERRY. I heard everything you said. You heard what I said, too, didn't you!

GWEN. Oh, Perry, we're not going to go all over this again, are we!

PERRY. No. We're not going all over it again. Not at all. We're not going over any of it again. It just comes down to one thing, that's all. *(Up stage slowly.)*

GWEN. It's like a bad dream! I can't go, Perry! Haven't I explained to you that I can't.

PERRY. Oh! . . . Yes. . . . Well, I've got to get started, of course, if I'm going to get there. Good-bye. *(He has been making a confused withdrawal. Hurt, angry. You hear the door bang.)*

(DOOR Slam.)

(GWEN *sits, her head up, defiantly. Then, as the realization of what has happened creeps upon her, she becomes less confident. Even terrified.* JULIE *appears on balcony from* FANNY'S *room. She is in hat and coat. She is first heard talking over her shoulder to* DEAN *and* KITTY, *who are unseen in the hallway off balcony.)*

JULIE. If he'd only try persuasion now and then instead of knocking people down right away. . . . *(Glances at her wrist watch.)* Good Lord! *(Com-*

ing down stairs, calls over the railing) Are you ready, Gwen?

DEAN. *(Entering)* Well, I'll be on my way, too.

KITTY. Where are you going?

JULIE. *(Descending the stairs. Sees that* GWEN *is not dressed for the street)* Good heavens, Gwen! Get your things on! What have you been doing? I must say you weren't much interested in Tony. *(Exit into library.)*

(FANNY *enters on balcony from center door. She is talking in a rather high-pitched voice to an unseen* TONY *in the room she has just left.)*

FANNY. Stay on the stage where you belong you wouldn't get mixed up with all that riff-raff! *(A mumble to herself as she stumps along the balcony and toward the stairs.)*

JULIE. *(From the library)* Is the car downstairs?

DEAN. *(Has gone up to alcove. Starts to plunge into his coat)* Drop me at the Lambs', Julie?

KITTY. *(Goes right)* You're late, aren't you? Lackaye'll be worried. *(Into her coat.)*

(TONY *enters from center door balcony, carrying a snow-shoe, singing a snatch of an aria. He is wearing a gay silk bathrobe, monogrammed, embroidered, tasseled. He advances with a romantic swing to the balcony rail. Reaching it, he strikes a magnificent pose aided by a high top-note.* FANNY *picks up the melody and carries it a phrase further.)*

JULIE. *(Re-enters from library, pulling on her gloves)* Lord, we're terribly late!

TONY. *(Shouts toward door right)* Jo, where the hell's my lunch!

JULIE. *(Making a last dash)* Gwen, *will* you get

your things on? . . . 'Bye, mother! . . . *(Kisses* FANNY.*)* Where do you want to go, Bert? . . . *(Cross right.)* See you later, Tony! . . . Gwen, what the devil's the matter with you! Why don't you come?

GWEN. I'm not coming.

*(*JULIE, *during this speech, has crossed almost to the alcove.* DEAN *is above her in the alcove doorway.* KITTY *has put on her coat and has crossed toward the piano.* FANNY *has dropped down left.* TONY *is sitting on balcony rail fixing the snow-shoe, surveying the departure of the others.)*

JULIE. *(Turns quickly, comes down a step or two)* Now, Gwen, don't start all that again. It's so silly.

GWEN. *(Rise)* I'm not going, do you understand! I'm not ever going. I'm not going to act in it at all.

JULIE. *(Impatiently)* Oh, for heaven's sake!

FANNY. Don't be sulky.

DEAN. My dear Gwen!

KITTY. What's the matter with her?

JULIE. Will you put on your hat and coat? *(Turns again as if to go.)*

GWEN. Listen to me! *(A note in her voice makes them realize that here is something serious)* I don't just mean I'm not going to be in this play. I'm not going to be in any play.

DEAN. What!

JULIE. My offspring has gone mad.

GWEN. I mean it. I'm through with the stage. I'm never going to act again.

JULIE. What are you talking about!

KITTY. She does mean it!

DEAN *and* FANNY. Not act again! Why—why—brrrrr—why—— The child's sick!

TONY. Don't go into pictures.

GWEN. Please! I've made up my mind, and all of you put together can't stop me. I'm through with the stage and I'll tell you why, if you want to know. I'm not going to have it mess up my whole life! *(An hysterical jumble of attempted explanation.)*

KITTY. What are you talking about?

JULIE. What do you mean, your whole life?

DEAN. What—what is this——

GWEN. *(Her talk is pierced from time to time by exclamations from the others of the family)* . . . Do you know what he did! He walked right out of the room. . . . If you think I'm going to give him up for a miserable little stage career just because we've always done it . . . we'd never see each other . . . he's get up in the morning and I wouldn't go to work till night. . . . Look at this afternoon with his mother waiting out there . . . it'll be like that for years and years. . . . You're not going to ruin my life. *(Tumbled explanation.)*

JULIE. What do you mean, ruin your life?

DEAN. What kind of talk is this?

KITTY. Ain't you ashamed of yourself——

GWEN. I'm going to marry Perry Stewart and be a regular person. And nothing you can say is going to stop me!

JULIE. *(Comes toward her)* I never heard such silly rot in all my life.

(From DEAN, FANNY, TONY, KITTY, *such lines as: "Why, it's preposterous! Quit and get married!")* (TONY. *"Who's Perry Stewart?")* (FANNY. *"Never thought I'd live to see this day.")*

JULIE. I don't know what you're talking about.

GWEN. Well, *I* know what I'm talking about. I'm sick of all this. I'm sick of being a Cavendish! I want to be a human being! *(From the others a shocked murmur.)*

FANNY. What's that!

DEAN. But you are a Cavendish!

JULIE. Of course you are.

GWEN. But I don't want to be! *(Crosses to sofa and sits.)*

JULIE. You've got to be! What do you think we've worked for all these years!

FANNY. You can't do this to us!

JULIE. My God! What anyone else would give for your chances!

DEAN. Yes!

FANNY. It's absurd!

JULIE. You can be the greatest of us all. Aubrey and Fanny Cavendish have just been stepping stones for you——

FANNY. What's that? What's that!

JULIE. Oh, Mother, please!

FANNY. I'll be a stepping stone for nobody! And as for Aubrey Cavendish, there's nobody since his day that can touch him. *(Cross to stairs.)*

(NOTE: *The following speeches overlap. Individual speeches carry no weight—it is the ensemble that counts. However, we do hear* KITTY *and* JULIE *say, "Well, if you want my opinion——" "Well, we don't want your opinion."*)

DEAN. One minute, please! *(Crosses to* FANNY*)* I believe my Macbeth——

GWEN. Listen to them! That's what I mean!

DEAN. Still takes rank as the finest interpretation of its day and age.

FANNY. You miserable upstart! Do you expect me to stand here and allow you to mention yourself and Aubrey Cavendish in one and the same breath? Aubrey Cavendish was an artist. He wouldn't have had you for his dresser. The greatest actors of his generation have sat at the feet of Aubrey Cavendish. Henry Irving, Beerbohm Tree, Richard Mansfield! And you have the presumption to fancy that your absurd struttings are comparable in any way with the histrionism of Aubrey Cavendish, the greatest actor that the English speaking stage has ever seen! And you stand there and tell me——

DEAN. *(Cue—"You miserable upstart"—)* Role for role, my dear Fanny, I'm a much better actor than Aubrey Cavendish ever dreamed of being. You must remember that his was the day of provinces, and while I have no doubt that he was a great favorite in the hamlets, it is quite another thing to win critical acclaim in London and New York. And you may recall that on three successive nights I played Othello, Iago and Petruchio. And that never under the historic roof of Wallack's Theatre have there been such three ovations, and a year later, at the old Vic, I——

JULIE. *(Cue—"Ever dreamed of being——") (Crossing to them)* For heaven's sake, you two! Telling how good you are! I'm pretty good myself, but you don't hear me talking about it!

KITTY. Well, if you want my opinion——

JULIE. *Well, we don't want your opinion!* This is purely a family matter, and it seems to me that you'll save yourself a good deal of trouble if you'll just keep out of it. *(To* DEAN) Oh, who cares which of you was the best actor! And, while we're about it, Herbert Dean, will you tell that wife of yours to stop talking. This is no concern of hers. Why doesn't she keep out of it? And why shouldn't Gwen be a greater actress than any of us! At least she's got intelligence on her side, and that's more than I can say for any of the rest of you. *(To* KITTY) Oh, all right! You're Bernhardt! You're Modjeska! You're Duse!

KITTY. *(Cue—"Don't want your opinion——")* No, I suppose not. Just because I am not one of your precious Cavendishes, I have no right to speak. But I want to tell you that Kitty LeMoyne can hold her head up with the best of them when it comes to acting. I may not have reached my present position by stepping on the heads of other people—— I've won out by talent and hard work. It isn't always the people who have their names in electric lights that are the best actors. I may not be a tradition in the theatre, but just the same——

(NOTE: *When* DEAN *says "in London and New York"* DELLA *enters from under stairs with* TONY'S *tray.)*

TONY. *(On seeing the tray)* Lunch!

CURTAIN.

TONY. *(Dashes down stairs)* Right over there, Della—— *(As the curtain descends.)*

(Tableaux.)

(The curtain goes—the argument is still raging—— TONY *is over right with his tray of food—* GWEN *still seated on the sofa. The telephone bell is ringing and* DELLA *answers the phone for the second*

CURTAIN.

ACT II

SCENE: *The scene is the same as in* ACT I.

The time is about six o'clock on the following afternoon, Saturday.

The table at the end of the sofa L. *is moved up by the piano. The armchair at the foot of stair is struck. A small bench now stands at the left of the sofa. A table above the door left contains considerable mail matter, a small vase to break stands on the table.*

There are fresh flowers in bowls and vases. Two of the lamps are lighted. The room is not yet fully lighted for the evening, however. The double doors leading into the library, left, are closed. The lamp on the commode is lighted.

AT RISE: *At the rise of the curtain there is heard the clash of fencing foils, the thud of feet, and male voices calling an occasional fencing term, sometimes in earnest, sometimes mockingly, "Have at thee, varlet!" in* TONY'S *voice.*

The library doors open. FANNY *enters. As she opens the doors she calls. She walks with her cane.*

(READY Lights Up.)

FANNY. Jo! *(She glances toward the balcony, from which comes the sounds of combat.)* Jo! *(Goes toward center, turns up lamp on piano. Shivers a little, draws about her a little shawl that hangs at her shoulders.* DELLA *enters right.)* Della, the fire's nearly out in the library.

DELLA. *(Over her shoulder)* Jo! Bring some wood—— *(Turns on lamp on secretary. A muffled answer from* Jo, *off.)*

FANNY. I must have dozed off. *(Another little shiver.)* What time is it, anyway?

DELLA. *(Tidying the rooms, picking up the papers, plumping cushions)* It's near six, I guess. Miss Julie's late. Said she was coming right home after the matinee. Course Saturday lots of young girls in the house, crowding back stage, taking her time up.

FANNY. More likely it's that passport of Tony's that's keeping her. Europe! Got to sail for Europe! Huh!

DELLA. One of those reporters tried to get up in the service elevator a little while ago, but they got him. *(Puts golf stick under arm.)*

FANNY. That crowd still standing around down there? In the wet snow? *(Crosses to window.)*

DELLA. There certainly is a mob of 'em. Jo says there's a bigger crowd than the time Mr. Tony got his first divorce.

(Clash! Clash! From the balcony the sounds of combat up there swell into an uproar as the battle grows hot. "Aha!" from TONY. *Shouted speech or two, unintelligible but loud, from the panting combatants.)*

DELLA. I wish Mr. Tony'd stop that fencing. Poor Miss Gwen feeling the way she does.

FANNY. Tony! Hush that racket! . . . He's carved his way through every room in the house this afternoon. I had to lock the door of my bathroom.

*(*Jo *enters from right. He carries an armful of fireplace wood.)*

Jo. Gee! Ought to see the crowd down there

now! And they just rolled up one of those trucks with a lot of lights on it. *(Crossing left.)*

DELLA. Good grief! What for?

JO. Going to take movies, I guess. Catch everybody, going in and out.

FANNY. They'll take no movies of me.

JO. And there's a fellow down there selling hot dogs and doing quite a business. . . . You want your tea, Mrs. Cavendish? *(Exits into library.)*

FANNY. Too near dinner time.

(The clash of foils comes up again. MCDERMOTT *and* TONY*, fencing, enter center of balcony, the former backing away from* TONY'S *attack.)*

DELLA. *(Going up stairs)* I brought a cup of tea up to Miss Gwen, but she wouldn't take it again.

FANNY. Still in her room, is she?

DELLA. Hardly eaten a mouthful in twenty-four hours.

(The combat leads across the balcony and down the stairs, TONY *maintaining the advantage, and keeping up at the same time a running comment, couched in a mixture of medieval and movie subtitle style.* JO *enters, watches the sword play.)*

TONY. Ha! He gives ground! Black Jennifer knows now the dark fate that soon is to o'ertake him. (DELLA *goes up stairs and breaks through the two swordsmen. She exits in* JULIE'S *room.)* Came the dawn, and yet they battled grimly upon the ancient parapet.

(JO *enters and watches the sword play.)*

MCDERMOTT. Je's! Go easy, there!

...irs) Ha! He begs for quarter! ... no mercy from Anthony the Ele-

..., the immortal passedo! the punto ...!"

..., ha, varlet! Thou didst not know, ...u didst hash a flagon of Burgundy from th... ...ou hadst run smack up against the nift-iest littl... wordsman in all of Gascony.

McDERMOTT. Hah!

TONY. And now, thou cur, prepare to meet thy end!

Prince, call upon the Lord!
I skirmish . . . feint a bit.
I lunge . . . I keep my word.
At the last line, I hit.

(He disarms McDERMOTT.*)*

JO. Hot dog!

TONY. Come, a kiss, my pretty wench! (FANNY *falls into* TONY'S *mood. Takes a few mincing steps to the victor's arms.)* For have I not won thee fairly! *(Turns his sword.)* Here, you are, Mac. I'll be up in a couple of minutes.

JO. I told you he was good. *(Exits into library.)*

McDERMOTT. *(Starts up stairs)* Yah! Gee!

(McDERMOTT *exit on balcony.)*

FANNY. You should have seen your father hold off eight of them—— What a swordsman—what an actor—— Aubrey and Fanny Cavendish in "A Gentleman of France." *(She works her way toward the stairs, her cane in one hand. She accompanies her next few lines with graphic illustration, in which the cane becomes the weapon.)* He'd send one head first right down the stairway, throw another one over the banister, quick as a wink he'd whirl and get one creeping up behind him—thrust—pierce—parry—exit—that scene alone took a full bottle of liniment every week. *(Sits on stairs.)*

TONY. *(Pats the withered cheek)* Those were the days, Fanny. *(Sits beside her.)*

FANNY. *(Sighs)* Those were the days.

(As FANNY, *nodding her head in reminiscent confirmation, turns away,* TONY *rolls down the sleeve of his shirt. A realization of the hour disturbs him.)*

TONY. Say, where the devil is Julie? What time is it, anyhow? It's late!

FANNY. Maybe the weather's delaying her. She rings down quarter to five.

TONY. Well, my God, is she getting my passport or isn't she? I've got to get out of here! I can't sail without a passport! She ought to know that!

FANNY. Now, now! Wolfe is helping her. You'll get it all right.

TONY. But when? The boat sails at midnight! I've got to get aboard early if I'm going to dodge that mob down there! *(A vague gesture toward the downstairs region)* I ought to crack a couple of them in the jaw—that's what I ought to do!

FANNY. You've done enough jaw cracking. How are you ever going to get past them anyhow, even if Julie does get you a passport?

TONY. Oh, the hell with them! *(Rises, goes* R.*)* I've got to get on that boat to-night! God! If Julie hasn't got that passport!

FANNY. *(With something of* TONY'S *fire)* Suppose she hasn't? Who says you've got to get on the boat? What for?

TONY. A million reasons! I feel like it! I want to get so far from Hollywood and sunshine—I never want to hear camera again! Or stage, either, for that matter! You can have it! I'm through! *(Comes* C.)

FANNY. Through! You've been saying that ever since "Fauntleroy."

TONY. I mean it this time! That's why I'm going abroad! *(Sits on bench* L. *of* C.) Give me two years in Munich with my violin under Ascher, and I'll show you what the stage means to me! I can be a great musician! Or I may go away into India with Krishnamurti and study Hindu philosophy! It's the only real thing in the world! You wear just one garment—a long white robe—and you eat just one food! Rice!

FANNY. That'll be restful!

TONY. *(Rises, goes* L.) The stage! I'd rather spend ten minutes in the Cathedral at Chartres—— I don't give a damn if I nev—— *(In the course of making a sweeping gesture he encounters the huge pile of letters on the table.)* What the hell is all this stuff? They've been here all day! What are they?

FANNY. *(Shouting at him)* They're for you! We've told you a dozen times! It's your mail we've been saving!

TONY. Well, why didn't you say so?

(He looks at it a moment—then he dumps them all into the waste basket, goes R.)

FANNY. *(Advancing on him)* Don't think you're fooling me about why you're going to Europe. Cathedrals, and violins, and rice! It's this Dago woman you're running away from. Else why was she on the train with you? *(She is center.)*

TONY. Oh, I'm not afraid of her. I gave her the slip at Chicago.

FANNY. Just the same, that's why you're going to Europe! Don't lie to me, Tony Cavendish!

TONY. *(Reluctantly giving ground)* Well, suppose I am! *(Flares up again)* Only I'm not afraid of her!

FANNY. Then what is it?

TONY. *(Paces a bit first)* It's that God damned process server she's got after me!

FANNY. What God damned process server?

TONY. *(It is being torn out of him)* The breach of promise suit.

FANNY. Breach of promise?

TONY. *(Scornfully)* Two hundred thousand dollars! She wants two hun—— *(On fire again.)* That's why I've got to stay cooped up here! You don't think I'm afraid of reporters, do you? But if they ever clap that paper on me I can't sail!

FANNY. Why wasn't I told of this? I suppose I was too young to know?

TONY. Fanny, darling——

FANNY. Keep away from me! Two hundred thousand for breach of promise. Assault and battery on this director—probably another hundred thousand. And breaking your contract with the picture company—— I guess half a million will cover it. *(Goes left.)*

TONY. It's worth it, I tell you! God, that sunshine! *(Throws himself on sofa.)*

FANNY. *(Back of sofa, fiercely)* What did you ever promise this movie actress that's worth two hundred thousand dollars?

TONY. Of, she claims to have some letters—— I didn't want her in the first place! She was Deming's girl! That's why he got sore! *(Lies on sofa.)*

FANNY. Who is she, anyhow? Where'd she come from?

TONY. Zeta Zaydak! She's a Pole.

FANNY. Look out for Poles!

(PHONE.)

(The phone bell rings. TONY *takes the receiver off*

the hook and listens for a second. Then he quietly puts the receiver down on the table; edges away.)

FANNY. A woman's voice?
TONY. No, but I'm not taking chances.
(AS He Hangs Up, Ring.)

(He goes back to the phone, a little furtiveness in his manner; takes up the receiver and listens again. Apparently he is satisfied that the caller is gone; he hangs up the receiver. Instantly the bell starts to ring again; TONY *quickly takes the receiver off again. Puts it once more on the piano; slides away quickly from the instrument. The sound of the outer door opening.)*
(DOOR Slam, JULIE.*)*

TONY. Who's that? *(The slam of the door.)*

*(*JULIE *enters. She has come in from the matinee. She is wearing smart winter street clothes—a luxurious fur coat and a costume to match. There is a bristling sort of vigor in the way she stations herself in the doorway.)*

JULIE. *(Talks as she enters)* Damn your dear public, Tony!
TONY. Did you get it?
JULIE. The entire population of New York is standing on the doorstep, howling for a glimpse of America's foremost screen lover. In the meantime they take what fortune sends, and it just so happened to be me.
FANNY. Your coat's ripped.
TONY. Julie! The passport! Have you got my passport?
JULIE. *(Calls)* What a dandy day this has been!

(Sits on sofa. DELLA *appears on balcony. Exits into* JULIE'S *room.)* . . . I had to get out at the corner—you don't dare drive up. And my dear Mrs. Cavendish, have you ever played to an audience made up entirely of sea lions! *(She is energetically tearing off hat, coat, kicks off her shoes.* DELLA, *meantime, comes down with mules. During* JULIE'S *speech she kneels and assists her with slippers, etc.)* They came in wet to the knees and never did dry off. They spent the first act taking galoshes off and the last act putting them on. *You* know—— *(Stoops to pull imaginary zippers.)* . . . I looked out once during the last act and couldn't see a face. And cough! I think they had a cheer leader. Lincoln couldn't have held them with the Gettysburg address. How's Gwen, mother? Is she better?

TONY. Now, look here, Julie!

JULIE. Shut up, Tony! . . . Has she eaten anything? What's she doing?

FANNY. No. Wouldn't take her tea.

JULIE. I'll go up.

DELLA. Dinner at the usual time, Miss Julie?

JULIE. No, hold it a while, Della.

DELLA. *(Edging toward door right, as she talks, delivering the day's messages in a sort of monotone)* Mr. Cartwright phoned, and Mrs. Blair's dinner's postponed till a week from Sunday, and——

JULIE. Not now, Della, please.

DELLA. And the La Boheme Shop says your dress is all ready. (DELLA *exits, right.)*

TONY. Dress be damned! My boat sails at midnight. What have you done about my passport!

JULIE. Tony, my love, Wolfe is bringing it.

TONY. He is? Why didn't you say so? Thank God! *(Sits chair* R.)

JULIE. He's been pulling all sorts of wires. He's been in and out of my dressing room all afternoon. *Everybody's* been in and out of my dressing room all afternoon. Compared to my dressing room, Grand Central Terminal was a rustic retreat. And all on account of you, my baby. Reporters, and process servers, and sob sisters. . . . I'm going up to Gwen.

FANNY. *(Detains her)* Gwen's all right. You lie down and take it easy—with another show to play.

TONY. Listen, Julie—how soon'll he get here?

JULIE. *(Lies on sofa)* Oh, I don't know. Right away. And he's bringing the money for you, too. They kept your reservation, and I've paid for it. You neglected to tell me that you were roughing it across in the royal suite.

TONY. I can't travel like a stowaway.

JULIE. Hire a battleship for all I care! But remember I'm a working girl. What do you do with all your money, anyway? You go out to Hollywood with a billion dollar contract and you buy a pink plaster palace for one hundred and fifty thousand, an Isotta Fraschini for twenty thousand and an Hispano Suiza for twenty-five, a camp in the Sierras for another fifty—good God, you were sunk a quarter of a million before they ever turned a crank on you! . . . And as soon as they start to take a picture you knock out the director and quit.

TONY. It'll all blow over in a month. That's why I want to get away.

JULIE. But why does it have to be Europe! What are you going to do when you get there!

FANNY. He's going to eat rice and play the violin.

TONY. I'm going to bathe in the pure beauty of Athens! I want to lose myself in the Black Forests of Bavaria! *(Cross to window.)*

FANNY. Mm! Switched your bookings.

TONY. I don't know where I'm going. Any place where it rains all the time.

(DOOR Bell.)

JULIE. All right. Go to Pago-Pago. But attend to

your own passport. I got my art to look after. *(Door bell rings.* TONY *dashes for stairs, turns.)*

JULIE. Keep calm. They can't get up here.

TONY. Think we'd better open it?

JULIE. You'll have to go out to catch the boat, won't you? They can't back the Aquitania up to the door.

TONY. I'll get out, all right, when the time comes. *(*Jo *enters, right. Starts toward outer door)* Wait, Jo! . . . *(To* JULIE*)* Maybe it's Wolfe, huh?

JULIE. Shoot from the hip, Jo.

JO. *(Genially)* Reminds me of the time the Grand Jury was after you. Remember that sheriff? *(In the alcove.* JULIE *sits up.)* When you took his gun away!

DEAN. What! What!

TONY. Keep a foot against the door!

JO. Who's out there?

DEAN. *(A muffled voice, off)* This is Herbert Dean!

JO. *(Opening door)* Oh, come right in, Mr. Dean.

(HERBERT DEAN *enters, with* JO *following him on. His entrance is marked by relieved sighs from* JULIE, FANNY *and* TONY.)

DEAN. They ought to be arrested, those fellows. *(Flicking from his garments the contaminating touch of those who had waylaid him on the sidewalk. This finished, he starts to remove his coat.* JO *takes it, with hat and stick.)* Pushing me all around.

TONY. You didn't tell them I was here?

DEAN. Of course not. But I hope, Anthony, that your next director will prove more congenial to you.

TONY. There isn't going to be any next director, old socks. . . . Come on, Jo. . . . I've got to pack and get out of here. *(Leaps up the stairs, followed by* JO.*)* Tell you what I want you to do. Want you to sneak out and get me three taxis exactly alike—and have them lined up in front of the door. . . . *(Exits center door balcony, with* Jo.)

DEAN. What the devil's he up to!

JULIE. Mother'll tell you. I'm going up to see Gwen.

DEAN. Wait—wait!

FANNY. I'm going in by the fire, Bertie, if you want to talk to me. *(Goes left.)*

DEAN. No—Julie—I want to talk to you. I've had a devil of a day. In the first place, where's Oscar? I gave him my play to read last night and I haven't been able to find him since. (JULIE *rises, goes to stairs.)*

FANNY. Isn't that funny! (FANNY *exits, library.)*

JULIE. He's coming here, Bert. Nail him. (JULIE *starts upstairs.)*

DEAN. Fine! Ah—just one thing more! *(Detaining her)* And this is what I really came about. *(Goes to her.)*

JULIE. Oh, Bert, not now, please.

DEAN. Now, hold on, Julie. I've got to talk to you. It's vital.

JULIE. Bert, can't it be some other time? I've simply got to see Gwen.

DEAN. No, no. I never needed you worse than I do now. I wouldn't tell this to anyone else, but I know you'll understand. Give me just a minute. Please!

JULIE. Why—what is it? What's the matter?

DEAN. You see, it's this way. These last five or six years I haven't—things haven't exactly—damn it all, it's youth! Youth! They write all the plays for young whipper-snappers! You've got to be built like a—uh—greyhound! Now mind you, I'm just as youthful as anybody. I keep in good condition. Try to. But it's impossible to get a good massage nowadays.

JULIE. Your figure's grand, darling.

DEAN. Not bad. But you see—I can't go around —sit in offices—they've got to come to me! I sit and wait for letters, rush to the telephone—think each time—first thing you know it's months and months——. What am I to do! *(Sits on sofa.)*

JULIE. Oh, you're just a little down. Something may come along any minute. *(Down to* DEAN, *arm on his shoulder.)*

DEAN. That's just it! I've got it! This play! It's a Godsend! Just what I need! It'll put me on my feet again. I can easily get in condition for it. Diet! Exercise!

JULIE. Yes, I know. I read it. It struck me then, that if instead of trying—if you'd be willing to play one of those attractive—uh—slightly greyed parts—

DEAN. Oh, I can get around that. Pink lights—and I don't look over thirty-five. But here is the real difficulty. It's the girl. She's got to be young—beautiful! A vision! I can't have—*(Very confidentially)* —To tell you the truth, Kitty will ruin it. She'll ruin *me!* She'll kill the first real chance I've had in years.

JULIE. But you know I can't do anything with her.

DEAN. But you can! That's just it. For God's sake, Julie, say you'll do it.

JULIE. Do what!

DEAN. Give her that part in your play—you know —the Colonel's wife. She'd be very good in that—

JULIE. But, Bert, I've got a good woman—— *(Going to stairs.)*

DEAN. *(Follows her, stands left of stairs)* Yes, yes—I know. But you could let that woman out. The point is, you're big enough, Julie. It wouldn't hurt your play. You're so admired, and popular—nothing can stop you. Now, I've never asked a favor before—little things, maybe—but we've always stood by each other—the family. Let me go and tell Kitty you suggested it.

JULIE. But I had Kitty once before, and——

DEAN. I know. But this will be different. She'll be very good in that part. . . . It means I am sure to have a hit. I could pay back everything I owe you—you, and different people——

JULIE. Oh, that's all right. Don't think of that now.

DEAN. *(Pats her hand, gratefully)* You're a brick, Julie. . . . You've been very kind—I hadn't meant to come to you again—but I wonder—I was going to ask if—you could spare another five hundred—just a few weeks——

(DOOR BELL, Three Rings.)

(Outer door bell rings sharply, three times.)

JULIE. That's Oscar.

DEAN. Oh! Splendid! Now, what do you say, Julie? Will you do that for me? Will you? (DELLA *enters—starts for door.)*

JULIE. *(Weakly)* Bert, I'll try to dig it up. I don't know—— Della, that's Mr. Wolfe. Tell him I'll be right down. I've got Gwen up here.

DELLA. *(Pausing on her way to the door)* How about dinner, Miss Julie?

JULIE. Oh, I can't right now, Della.

DELLA. It's getting late.

JULIE. I don't know what to say about Kitty, Bert. (DELLA *exit to outer door.)* You've given me an awful problem. Fortunately I've got so many that one more doesn't matter.

DEAN. Then you will do it, huh? Good!

JULIE. Good! Hell, it's perfect. *(Exits center door balcony.)*

WOLFE. *(As* DELLA *opens the door for him)* Say, what a mob scene you got down there!

DELLA. It certainly is terrible, all right.

WOLFE. *(Entering on this speech)* And what's more, it's bad publicity.

(Sees DEAN, *breaks off. From his look in* DEAN'S *direction he is plainly far from delighted.* DELLA *follows. Waits to receive* WOLFE'S *coat.)*

DEAN. Ah, Oscar, my boy!

WOLFE. Oh, hello.

DEAN. This is fortunate!

DELLA. Miss Julie'll be right down. Shall I take your coat?

WOLFE. No, thanks. I don't stay.

(FANNY *appears in doorway, left. She is carrying a manuscript of a play.)*

FANNY. Hello, Wolfe! I thought it was your voice. (DELLA *goes out right.)*

WOLFE. *(Up)* Your gifted daughter, Mrs. Cavendish, certainly gave a fine ham performance this afternoon.

FANNY. Did you get his passport?

WOLFE. Well, I want to talk to Julie about it. Where is she?

FANNY. She's up with Gwen.

WOLFE. Yah? How is Gwen? Come to her senses yet?

FANNY. Stubborn as ever. *(Comes down. Sits on sofa.)*

WOLFE. She'll come around.

DEAN. Now, Oscar, I've got a dinner engagement. *(Going to* OSCAR. *His watch.)* Tell me how the play impressed you. Wonderful, isn't it? Tremendous!

WOLFE. *(Hesitatingly)* M-m-m, yes—but——

DEAN. I knew you'd be crazy about it! *(Goes to*

hallway.) Now, I'll start lining up a cast and come in to see you to-morrow. About what time, say?

WOLFE. I don't know—— Oh—uh—any time.

DEAN. *(A dignified scamper up to the alcove, throws his coat over his arm, claps on his hat, takes his stick)* That's fine! Fine! We can start rehearsals in about ten days, eh? *(Picks up hat and coat.)*

WOLFE. *(Strolls uneasily up toward alcove)* Now, not so fast, Dean. Pretty heavy show you got there. Take a pile of money to put that on.

DEAN. *(In protest)* Oh, no, no, no, no.

WOLFE. No, no, no—— Yes, yes, yes. Fourteen scenes. Grand Central Terminal, Garden of Eden—

DEAN. Just a few drapes. *(Exits hallway.)*

OSCAR. Court of King Solomon—Battle of Waterloo——

(The door is heard to slam. WOLFE *comes down, puffing at his cheeks in rather stunned perplexity. His eye roves to* FANNY, *a grim figure in her chair. The two are in accord.)*

FANNY. I think Bertie has retired and doesn't know it.

WOLFE. I wish they were all like you, Fanny. *(Comes over to pat her shoulder)* What d'you think? Going to be able to troupe again after the Holidays?

FANNY. Tried to tell you yesterday, but you were so busy with your English playwrights.

WOLFE. Say, if I had to pick one actress out of the whole caboodle of 'em, you know who it'd be. Come on, tell me. Think you can start out again? Sure enough?

FANNY. You can dust off the "Castlemaine" scenery, and I'd just as soon you'd route me to the Coast.

WOLFE. 'At a girl! *(Crosses left.)* You're worth a dozen of these New-York-run actresses. No foolishness about you. No private cars and maids in the contract, and telegrams from the company manager you won't go on because the theatre's cold. No, sir! You're the girl that does twenty-eight hundred in Boise City, Idaho, and catches the six-fourteen next morning for Pocatello.

FANNY. I did twenty-nine hundred in Boise City.

WOLFE. Chairs in the aisles, h'm? I tell you, if Bert—*(A gesture toward the departed figure)*—had taken his hits out on the road he wouldn't be in this jam to-day. But by nature Bertie is a Lambs' Club actor, and look what happens! In a couple more years he'll own six toupees, and be playing Baron Stein in an all-star revival of Diplomacy.

FANNY. *(Getting to her feet to take the oath)* May God strike me dead if I ever appear in an all-star revival!

(She sits again. Then JULIE *enters on balcony from center door. Starts downstairs.)*

JULIE. Well, she's promised to dress and come out of that room, anyhow. That's more than she's done all day.

WOLFE. Say, what kind of a show are you going to give tonight, with all this hullabaloo!

JULIE. Once Tony goes, things will be a little better. It's so restful to think that at midnight he'll be rounding Sandy Hook.

WOLFE. M-m, that's what I came to talk about.

JULIE. *(Alarmed)* What!

WOLFE. It don't go so quick. These fellows——

JULIE. You don't mean you can't get it! Oh!

WOLFE. Well, now, hold on. I don't say I can't yet exactly. There seems to be some sort of monkey business going on. Maybe they got wind of something and don't want him to get away.

JULIE. Oscar, another twenty-four hours with this

caged lunatic and you can order straight-jackets for two. He's impossible to live with—and those terrible people on the street!

WOLFE. Now, now, now! Did Oscar ever fail you? We'll get it all right—I hope. Anyhow, here's his money. That's that much. *(Cross* R.C.)

FANNY. *How* much?

JULIE. What's the difference, Mother? He has to have it. *(Tosses money on piano.)* Oscar, I owe you a ghastly lot of money, don't I? How much?

WOLFE. The money you're welcome to, Julie. But it oughtn't to be that you got to come to me like this. You make as much money as any woman in the business. What the devil do you do with all your money, anyhow!

JULIE. Why—I don't know. What do you mean—do with it?

FANNY. What does anybody do with it?

WOLFE. Well, just for argument's sake, let me ask you once! Forty-one weeks. Fifteen hundred a week. You've made sixty thousand since you opened in this play, and that says nothing about all the other ones. In the past twenty years, I bet you, you made a million dollars. Now how much of it have you actually got?

JULIE. Let's see—where's my bag? I've got over three dollars in that, and Della owes me seventy-five cents—— (Jo *enters on balcony; starts to descend stairs.)* Oh, I don't know, Oscar. It just goes. *(To* Jo, *who is crossing to the door at right)* Jo, tell Della caviar for Miss Gwen's dinner.

Jo. Yes, Miss Julia. *(Goes right.)*

JULIE. *(To* WOLFE *and* FANNY) Perhaps that'll tempt her.

WOLFE. Well. *(Quick little gesture and a squeeze of* FANNY'S *hand.)* I stayed longer than I meant to. *(Starts up to alcove.)* I let you know the minute I see this fellow, huh?

JULIE. *(Following him up a step or two)* Oscar, you're an angel! Would it interest you to know that you are adored by the most beautiful actress on the American stage?

WOLFE. *(Airily)* Nope.

JULIE. My Galahad!

FANNY. Goodbye, Wolfe. (WOLFE *goes hallway. The slam of the door.)*

(DOOR Slam.)

JULIE. Gwen! . . . Oh, I hope he gets that passport! I don't dare tell Tony there's any doubt of it —let's just hope he gets it—— Gwen! *(A second's vain pause for an answer.)* She promised she'd come down.

FANNY. I thought she'd get tired of moping in her room like Elsie Dinsmore.

JULIE. Gwen, dear! *(Goes to stairs.)*

GWEN. *(Heard upstairs)* Yes, mother.

JULIE. Aren't you coming down, dear? I wish you would.

GWEN. *(Off)* Yes, mother.

FANNY. Who is this What's-his-name of hers, anyway? Doesn't seem to me like anything but an average young man.

JULIE. They're all average young men.

FANNY. Speaking of average, how's Mr. Gilbert Marshall? Have you seen him yet?

JULIE. No. I suppose when he telephoned yesterday, and they told him I was out, he just thought I didn't want to see him. Perhaps it's just as well. It's a long time ago, and he's probably bald, and fat, and talks about conferences.

(GWEN *appears on the balcony. She is in one of those chiffon negligees; there is something of the Ophelia about her appearance. She has been cooped up with her resolution for twenty-*

four hours, and it's beginning to wear her down.)

GWEN. *(Advancing to the rail)* Nobody else there, is there?

(GWEN *comes slowly, pensively, down the stairs.)*

JULIE. Only your aged relatives.
FANNY. Speak for yourself.

(GWEN *has come down.)*

JULIE. (FANNY *is seated on sofa* R. JULIE *is to sit on bench* L. *of sofa.* GWEN *is between them on sofa)* Do you want to sit here, dear? Or shall we go in by the fire?
GWEN. *(Sits)* Oh, this is all right. *(Glances up with a rather wan smile.)* I don't mean to act like a prima donna. I just feel like hell, that's all.
JULIE. *(Standing over her)* I know you do, dear. I hate to see you unhappy like this. *(Leans over, kisses the top of her head lightly.)* But you have so little sense.
GWEN. *(Her lip quivering. Very low)* He didn't even telephone. He might at least have telephoned.
FANNY. How do you know he didn't? Tony had the receiver off most of the day.
JULIE. *(Puts receiver back on hook)* Yes.
GWEN. *(Eagerly)* Do you think so! He might have, mightn't he? Oh! *(A little whimper of dismay. She even weeps, weakly.)*
JULIE. *(Pats her shoulder tenderly)* Now, Gwen.
GWEN. Oh, Mother, I love him so!
JULIE. There's nothing to cry about. *(A hand on her shoulder, patting her into calm)* There! *(A moment's pause while* GWEN *grows quieter.)*

FANNY. You can love him and marry him, too, can't you?

JULIE. Of course you can marry him, Gwen, and live happy ever after.

FANNY. Only why you think you have to quit the stage to do it is more than I can figure out.

JULIE. It's hard for us to realize that you wouldn't want to keep on, Gwen.

FANNY. Your mother and I both got married. But we didn't drop more important things to do it.

GWEN. There isn't anything more important.

FANNY. Fiddlesticks! Marriage isn't a career. It's an incident! Aubrey Cavendish and I were married in the Church of St. Mary Redcliffe, in Bristol, England, just before the matinee. The wedding super was served on the stage of the Theatre Royale between the matinee and the night performance—we played "She Stoops to Conquer" in the afternoon, and "A Scrap of Paper" was the night bill. They sent the supper in from the George and Lion next door, and very nice it was, too, but I remember they'd gone and put nutmeg in the gooseberry tarts, and Aubrey never could abide nutmeg. It must have been that that upset him, for he gave the only bad performance that night that I ever saw him give.

GWEN. I know, Grandma. But that's got nothing to do with me. You married an actor, and—*(Turning to her mother, swiftly)*—so did you. You lived the same sort of lives.

JULIE. Oh, I knew some rather nice men who weren't actors—didn't I, Fanny? *(A gesture from* FANNY *of utter dismissal of this subject as being too vast and agonizing to go into.)* There were lots of times when I thought that being a wife and mother was all that mattered in the world. And then each time I'd learn all over again that that wasn't *enough* for me.

FANNY. I should say not.

JULIE. Earthquakes, and cyclones, and fire and flood, and somehow you still give the show. I know it says in the contract that you stop for "acts of God," but I can't remember that I ever did. *(Rise.)*

FANNY. Nor I. Nor your grandfather. Nobody ever knew what a sick man Aubrey Cavendish was, those last months. But he played a full season of thirty-five weeks. Dropped dead on the stage of Macauley's in Louisville two minutes after the curtain fell on Saturday night, the week we closed. Not only that, but he waited to take four calls.

GWEN. I know, I know. *(Rises—goes* R.*)* But—I'm not like that, that's all. *(Sits near window.)*

JULIE. *(Rises, crosses to* GWEN*)* You think you're not, but you are! Marry him if you love him, Gwen, but don't give up everything to do it! The day might come when you'd hate him for it.

GWEN. Hate Perry! *(A little bitter, scornful laugh.)* You just don't know what you're talking about.

JULIE. Gwen, do you think it's going to be any fun for me to have them see you step out—acting with me in my play, and, for all I know, walking away with it! You'll be so fresh, and such a surprise! And it'll be your night. I'll be very proud and happy, of course. *(A very little pause, and then, almost as though to convince herself)* . . . of course. They'll say, "That's her daughter." But ten years from now it'll be, "That's her mother."

GWEN. I'll never be half the actress you are.

JULIE. Gwen, if I could only make you realize that the thrill you get out of doing your work is bigger than any other single thing in the world! *(A little gesture of protest from* GWEN.*)* Oh, I know! There's love. But you can be the most fortunate person in the world, Gwen. You can have both. But for God's sake don't make the mistake of giving up one for the other.

FANNY. No, child!

GWEN. Work! Acting isn't anything. What's acting compared to——

FANNY. It's everything. It's work and play and meat and drink. They'll tell you it isn't—your fancy friends—but it's a lie! And they know it's a lie! They'd give their ears to be in your place. Don't make any mistake about that.

JULIE. There'll be plenty of things that you'll have to give up—gay things and amusing things—I've missed dinners—(DELLA *appears in doorway right, evidently meaning to get* JULIE'S *attention)*—and parties and rides and walks and——

FANNY. What is it, Della?

DELLA. How about dinner?

FANNY. Don't bother us! (DELLA *exits, slowly and unobtrusively, puzzled. Stealing* JULIE'S *thunder)* Yes, you've got to leave, and go down to a stuffy dressing room and smear paint on your face and go out on the stage and speak a lot of fool lines, and you love it! You love it! You couldn't live without it! Do you suppose I could have stood these two years, hobbling around with this thing—*(Brandishing her cane)*—if I hadn't known I was going back to it!

JULIE. Long as I've been on the stage there isn't a night when I stand in the wings waiting for my cue that I don't get that sick feeling at the pit of my stomach. And my hands are cold and my cheeks are hot, and you'd think I'd never been on the stage before.

FANNY. Yes, yes! That's it! Every night when I'm sitting here alone I'm really down there at the theatre. Seven-thirty, and they're going in the stage door. Good evening to the doorman. Taking down their keys and looking in the mail rack. Eight o'clock! The stage hands are setting up. *(Raps with her cane.)* Half hour, Miss Cavendish! Grease paint, rouge, mascara. Fifteen minutes, Miss Cavendish! My costume. . . . More rouge. . . . Where's the rabbit's foot! . . . Overture! . . . Good evening, everybody. . . . How's the house tonight? . . . The curtain's up! . . . Props! . . . Cue. . . . Enter. *(Rise.)* That's all that's kept me alive these two years. If you weren't down there for me, I wouldn't want to live. . . . I couldn't live. You . . . down there . . . for me . . . going on . . . going on . . . going on. . . .

(The excitement and the strain are too much for her. Suddenly she goes limp, topples, crumples. JULIE *and* GWEN, *standing near her, catch her as she is about to fall, and place her in the chair from which she has risen. She is briefly unconscious.)*

JULIE. Mother! Mother, what's the matter!

GWEN. Grandma! Grandma!

JULIE. Jo! Tony! Della! Quick!

GWEN. *(At* FANNY'S *side, frantic and remorseful)* It's all right, grandma. I'll do it. I will. I will! Grandma! I'll do it.

(JO *and* DELLA *enter.* JO *picks up* FANNY, *places her on sofa.)*

JULIE. Some water—whisky—quick!

(MCDERMOTT *appears on balcony, followed by* TONY, *in answer to* JULIE'S *calls.* JO *dashes off after a flask.* MCDERMOTT *comes down to assist* JO.)

TONY. What's the matter? What is it?

JULIE. She fainted! We were talking!

TONY. Do something! For God's sake, do something! What are you all standing around for! Where is everybody? *(On stairs.)*

GWEN. It's all my fault! Grandma! Grandma!

(JO *enters swiftly, with flask. Ad libs. Exclamations, suggestions, broken speeches from group. "She's coming around." "She's better." "There, mother." "It's me, mother. It's Julie." "Telephone the doctor." "You're all right. You're all right, mother." "You're all right now." "There, take that, mother. Just a sip. You'll be fine in a minute. There. She's taking it. Moisten her forehead with it," etc.)*

TONY. Mother! Mother! It's me—Tony. *(The confused murmur of talk slowly dies.)*

GWEN. I'm going to do it, Grandma. I didn't mean it. I will! Of course I will!

JULIE. Did you hear? It's all right! Everything's going to be all right!

TONY. She's better now! Aren't you, mother?

FANNY. *(Struggles rather feebly to rise; to assert her independence. Her voice is little more than a whisper)* I'm all right. There's nothing the matter. But I think I'll go up and lie down. *(They gather round to assist her.)*

JULIE. Jo, get a hot water bag. Della, run ahead and turn the bed down.

TONY. Let me alone. I've got her.

(JO *and* DELLA *run up the stairs ahead of the others.* DELLA *exits into* FANNY'S *room, the first door on the balcony.* JOE *exits in* JULIE'S *room.)*

MCDERMOTT. That's the stuff. Just lean on me. You're doing swell.

TONY. Here we go! Now!

JULIE. Careful, Tony. Slow. *(They move cau-*

tiously up the stairway.) She oughtn't to be walking up stairs.

TONY. She won't let me carry her.

FANNY. *(They are half-way up the stairs)* Wait a minute. . . . Wait. . . .

JULIE. What is it! Mother, do you feel faint again?

FANNY. I just want to rest a minute. . . . Just a minute. . . . *(A long sigh.* MCDERMOTT *is on her left.* TONY, *as she pauses and turns, a step below her, on her right.* JULIE *is a step behind her.* GWEN, *her back to the audience, is about at the foot of the stairs.)* No use . . . No use fooling myself. . . . I'm through. . . . I'll never go back again. It's finished. (FANNY *faints.)*

MCDERMOTT. Look out there! (TONY *catches her up in his arms and starts up with* FANNY.) You better get a doctor.

(JO *comes hurrying out of the center door carrying a hot water bag, goes swiftly into* FANNY'S *room left.)*

JULIE. How white she is. *(They stream into the bedroom.* JULIE *is heard giving orders to* DELLA. GWEN, *during the latter part of this scene, has taken a few slow steps up the stairs, so that she is by now about half-way up. The movement of the door's closing finds her quite still on the stairs. She brings her hands together in a little gesture of desperation. You hear the impact of her closed fist against her palm. Stumbles on up, heavily. Exits, center. Off)* Spirits of ammonia. Bring the whole thing. (JO *exits hurriedly into* JULIE'S *room.)*

(NOTE: *The following conversation is heard in* FANNY'S *room, and continues until* JULIE *enters and talks to* GIL.)

JULIE. Look out! That's hot! Put it at her feet.
FANNY. I hate hot water bags——
TONY. Here. This'll pick you up.
JULIE. Give it to me. Let me do it. Just a sip, darling.
MCDERMOTT. Why'n't you open a window?
JULIE. No. Her hands feel so cold.
FANNY. Stop this clatter or I'll get right up.
JULIE. Just you dare, Fanny Cavendish!
TONY. That stuff's no good. Swig of whisky's the thing.
FANNY. I won't drink it.
GWEN. Oh, what a bad girl you are!
JULIE. Darling, are you all right now.
(AS Della Comes Down Stairs. Door Bell.)

(DELLA *follows* JO *into* FANNY'S *room, goes downstairs.* JO *enters from* JULIE'S *room, carrying a heavy medicine case.)*

DELLA. *(Calls up to* JO) I'll go. (JO *goes on into* FANNY'S *room.* DELLA *goes to outer door.)*
GILBERT MARSHALL. *(Off)* Miss Cavendish in? Miss Julie Cavendish?
DELLA. Yes, sir.
GIL. Will you tell her—Mr. Gilbert Marshall? (DELLA *reappears from alcove a little ahead of* GIL.)
DELLA. Yes, sir, if you'll just—— I'll ask her if she can see you. *(Exits under stairs.)*

(GILBERT MARSHALL *enters at* DELLA'S *exit. He is forty-seven, quiet, dominant, successful. He gives the effect of power and control. Hair slightly graying. Very well dressed. He is in topcoat now as he stands surveying the charming empty room. His hat and stick in his hand. As* JO *opens the door to* FANNY'S *room, there comes from it a chorus of high-pitched voices.*

MARSHALL *has come down so that he is now somewhat right of center. At the sound of what evidently is a scene upstairs he turns and surveys the balcony. There is something of recognition in his glance and manner as he hears this. After a moment* MCDERMOTT *rushes hurriedly out of center door, balcony. He goes to* TONY'S *room.* JO *comes out. He comes down the stairs.* MCDERMOTT *enters carrying bottle of alcohol. He goes to* FANNY'S *room.* JO *glances inquiringly at* GILBERT MARSHALL.)

GIL. Is there something the matter? Is Miss Cavendish?

JO. It's Mrs. Cavendish, sir.

GIL. Oh, I'm sorry. (DELLA *enters from servants' quarters carrying a glass. She exits upstairs in* FANNY'S *room. The sound of voices is heard again.)* Maybe I'd better not wait.

JO. Oh, she's all right now. Just a kind of fainting spell.

GIL. I won't intrude now. Just say I'll telephone.

JO. I'm sure Miss Julie'll be right down.

GIL. *(Doubtfully)* Well——

JO. Just be seated, sir. (JO *exits under stairs.)*

(GIL *stands a moment, uncertainly. The door of* FANNY'S *room opens from the inside. No one is to be seen in the doorway, but* FANNY'S *voice is heard, high-pitched and querulous.)*

FANNY. *(From off)* Fiddlesticks—go to bed in the middle of the day!

(GIL *picks up gloves from table where he has laid them, puts on hat, starts toward outer door.* JULIE *comes out of* FANNY'S *room quickly. A small towel is pinned across the front of her gown. Her hair is somewhat dishevelled. One sleeve is rolled up. She sees* GIL *about to depart.)*

JULIE. *(Down the stairs swiftly)* Gil! Gil! Don't go!

GIL. Julie! *(Comes quickly to foot of stairs)* Can I help? What's wrong?

JULIE. It's nothing. I'm—it's just—— *(Begins to cry—helplessly. Clings to him, a refuge.)*

GIL. I'm so sorry. Is she very ill? I shouldn't have come, should I?

JULIE. I'm so ashamed. I don't know why I—— She's all right now. She's perfectly all right. It's been such a hellish day. Everything in the world that could happen—— Gil, you're still sane, aren't you?—and solid, and reliable, and sure!

GIL. I hope so.

JULIE. How nice! . . . *(Suddenly aware of her appearance. Glances down at towel)* And I was going to be so ravishing on our first meeting. I had it all planned. *(Unpins towel. Throws it aside)* Let me make another entrance, will you? I'll say, "It's really you, Gil! After all these years!" And you'll say——

GIL. *(One stride, takes her hand)* I'll say——

(DELLA *enters on balcony from* FANNY'S *room. The sound of the door interrupts* GIL. *Both glance up quickly.)*

JULIE. Do you want me, Della?

DELLA. *(Comes swiftly down the stairs)* No, she's fine, Miss Julie. Mr. Tony's telling her stories about Hollywood to quiet her. *(Exits under stairs.)*

GIL. Julie, I know I'm in the way. I—— *(Goes right.)*

JULIE. Oh, please stay, Gil. This is the first peaceful moment I've had to-day.

GIL. No wonder, with that mob downstairs.

(DELLA *enters.)*

JULIE. You've seen the papers, of course.

DELLA. Pardon me, Miss Julie, but it's twenty minutes after seven. I thought perhaps—— *(An apprehensive glance at* GIL. *Dinner is on* DELLA'S *mind.)*

JULIE. It's all right, Della. Never mind. I'll let you know.

DELLA. Yes, ma'am. *(Goes under stairs. A moment's silence as the two are alone. They look at each other. Then they speak together.)*

GIL *and* JULIE. You haven't changed a bit. *(A light laugh as they realize the absurdity of this.)*

GIL. Do you know, Julie, I haven't gone to see you once in all these years?

JULIE. I think I'd have felt it if you'd been out front. And you never were? *(Sits on sofa.)*

GIL. No. I've only been in New York a few times since then. South America's a long way off. But I kept track of you. I took the New York Times and —the Theatre Magazine, is it?

JULIE. You haven't been exactly hidden from the public gaze, Gil. What was it you found down there? Radium—lying around in chunks?

GIL. Oh, no, not radium. Platinum. *(Sits on sofa.)*

JULIE. Anyhow, you've got millions and millions.

GIL. I've done—pretty well. But say! You're certainly top of the heap in your line.

JULIE. Oh, the Zenith!

GIL. And you have a daughter, haven't you? Seventeen.

JULIE. That was last year's paper. Gwen's eighteen.

GIL. I want so much to see her.

(PHONE.)

JULIE. We're going to be in a play together for the first time. Think of it!

GIL. That ought to be exciting.

(PHONE.)

JULIE. It's been exciting enough. Gwen got a sudden horrible idea that—— *(The telephone rings.* JULIE *glances quickly toward door right, as though expecting* DELLA *to answer. Goes to telephone.* GIL *rises, goes* R.*)* Hello! *(*GIL *removes overcoat—places it* R.*)* Yes . . . Oh, Oscar! . . . Oh, dear! . . . Yes, I'm sure you did, but—— Oh, Oscar! *(*TONY *enters balcony from* FANNY'S *room, carefully closing door behind him, his attention all on the telephone below.)* Well, of course, if you can't, there's no use—— There's nothing to be . . . Yes, I know it is. I'm leaving right away . . . Don't worry. I'll give a swell performance. *(Hangs up.)*

TONY. Was that Wolfe? *(Comes down stairs.)*

JULIE. Oh, Tony! . . . How's mother? All right?

TONY. Asleep. . . . Who was that on the phone? Wolfe, wasn't it?

JULIE. Now, Tony, I don't want you to hit the ceiling——

TONY. *(With a snarl)* He hasn't got it!

JULIE. It's not so vital. You haven't done anything so terrible——

TONY. You don't know what you're talking about! You'll find out if it's vital! Why, my God! If this woman——

JULIE. Oh, don't be childish, Tony! What can she do to you? You talk like somebody in a melodrama! Now calm down and shut up. . . . Gil, this is my brother Tony.

TONY. What can she do to me? I'll tell you what she can do to me! She can——

JULIE. Tony, will you be quiet? This is Mr. Gilbert Marshall. Gil, my brother Tony.

TONY. *(Through his teeth)* Charmed! . . . *(Turns again to* JULIE*)* What the hell kind of a jam do you think I'm in, anyway? *(During the following speech he is down the stairs, up and down the room furiously, up the stairs again, and into center door balcony)* What do you think I blew all the way from California for! The ride! I've got to get out of here, I tell you! Zaydak's in town by this time. Do you know what that means! You don't know that Polecat! Why, I've seen her pick up a—— *(Snatches a fragile glass ashtray off the table, which he uses to accent his gestures as he goes on, forgetting meanwhile that he has it)* She's a killer! She'll do anything! She'd just as soon shoot as look at you. She's a Pole. She's cuckoo about me, and she knows I'm through with her. Now if you don't want to do anything to help me, why, all right. *(Turns, starts upstairs)* You're a Hell of a sister—I'm only your brother and why should you bother about me! But I'm telling you now, if they get me I'll be all over the front page, and so will you, and so will Gwen, and the whole damned family! Now if that's what you want, believe me, you're going to get it! *(On the balcony, discovers ornament still in his hand. A smothered exclamation of disgust at finding it. Smashes it to the floor)* . . . Pleased to have met you, Mr. Gilson. *(Exits, balcony—left.)*

(A moment's pregnant pause. GIL *stands looking up after the departed whirlwind. His gaze comes back to* JULIE.*)*

GIL. Is he always like that?

JULIE. Oh, no. That's the brighter side.

GIL. But what is it he wants? What didn't you do for him?

JULIE. He wants to sail to-night on the Aquitania, and we can't get a passport.

GIL. A passport? And he's putting you through all this for a—— Well, no wonder you're upset.

JULIE. This! What you've seen is practically the rest hour. We've had Gwen deciding to leave the stage forever——

GIL. What!

JULIE. —Mother having a little collapse. Uncle Herbert—you remember Uncle Herbert, don't you? Well, we won't go into that.

GIL. Look here, Julie. When does Tony want to sail? *(Cross to phone.)*

JULIE. Midnight. The Aquitania. (GIL *goes directly to the telephone, takes up the receiver)* Why? Gil, do you mean you know someone that can——

GIL. Bowling Green ten-five-one-six . . . How soon can he get down there?—Tony, I mean.

JULIE. Why—right away, I guess, if he can slip by the reception committee.

GIL. Tell him to get ready—no, wait a minute—Hello! John? . . . Let me talk to Moran. . . .

JULIE. Gil, do you mean you can get it? Oh, if you only could!

GIL. Don't you know there isn't anything in the world that I wouldn't . . . Hello! . . . Why, if I thought you needed me, Julie, I'd go to the ends of the . . . Hello! Moran? This is Marshall. . . . Now get this. . . . I want an emergency passport Aquitania to-night . . . That's right . . . I want you to meet me on the Cunard dock in half an hour. *(To* JULIE*)* Can he make it in half an hour?

JULIE. *(Eagerly)* Yes, yes!

GIL. *(In phone)* Now, no slip-up on this.

JULIE. *(Sotto voce)* Twenty minutes.

GIL. *(In there)* I'll give you the details when I see you . . . Right. *(Hangs up.)*

JULIE. Oh, Gil!

GIL. I'll meet Tony and smuggle him on board. Moran will do the rest.

JULIE. *(Goes to stairway; even mounts a step or two)* Tony! Tony! *(Turns to* MARSHALL*)* It's wonderful of you, Gil. Why, you're one of these strong, silent men, aren't you! (TONY *enters from door left, balcony.)* Tony, we've got it. Hurry up! Get ready!

TONY. What! You mean the passport!

JULIE. Yes! Yes! Gil got it for you. He's going to meet you there and fix——

TONY. *(Racing down the stairs)* Whee! *(A leap)* That's the stuff! *(Bounds over to* JULIE*)* You're a swell sister!—Jo! Jo!

JULIE. Now, Tony, you understand, you're to go right down there. Gil will meet you on the dock. He'll have the passport.

(JO'S *head is seen in doorway, right.)*

JO. Yes, sir.

TONY. Jo, I'm going to leave in five minutes. You got everything ready?

JO. Yes, sir. It will be.

TONY. All right. Go to it. *(Leaps for the stairs as* JO *exits)* Sis, you're a grand kid! I knew I could count on you. Old reliable. *(To* GIL, *who has crossed left)* Much obliged, old fellow! *(To* JULIE, *in the same breath)* Who is he, anyway? *(Exits, on balcony left.)*

JULIE. *(Groping uncertainly for a chair. Rather mockingly utters the trite phrase of the theatre to cover her own shaken condition)* Won't you—sit down? *(Sits on sofa.)*

GIL. Why do you stand for all this?

JULIE. Oh, Tony doesn't mean anything. He's always like that.

GIL. What do you mean? That you have this kind of thing all the time, and that you go ahead and put up with it?

JULIE. Oh, sometimes families are . . . It just happens to-day that blood is thicker than usual.

GIL. But these other things that you were talking about. You oughtn't to allow them to do that! You're a successful actress. Head of your profession! You ought to be the one they're running around for. And look! Everybody dumping their troubles on you.

JULIE. Oh, it isn't always like this.

GIL. *(Sits on small bench left of sofa)* You know, Julie, the reason I went away was so that you could go ahead and be an actress. All that stuff about Cavendish, and the stage being your real life, and the only way you could be happy. Well, you've got everything you went after. And how about it? Are you happy?

JULIE. Happy! I don't know.

GIL. Of course you're not, Julie. I've stayed away all these years because I thought at least you were living the life you wanted most. And then I come back and find this. You ought to have everything in the world. You ought to have everything done for you—done for you by some one who loves you . . .

JULIE. Oh, don't, Gil—don't say things that will make us both——

GIL. Don't you know what you ought to be doing instead of this? The way you ought to be living! Why, you ought to be in a country house somewhere, with a garden around it, and trees. Julie, if you could see the place I've got in England. An old stone house, and a rose garden that's famous. It's a beautiful place, Julie; and there it stands, empty.

JULIE. Oh, Gil!

GIL. Or we can go any place else you want—Cairo, St. Moritz—anywhere you say. Don't you know that's the way you ought to be living! Don't you?

JULIE. *(Rises)* I don't know! I don't know!

GIL. Julie! *(Takes her in his arms)* What fools we've been! What fools!

JULIE. Gil—wait! Let me think a minute. Let me get my breath.

GIL. You've had too long to think. It's settled.

JULIE. *(As she gently frees herself)* No—please! I'm not quite sure what's happened. I can't think very clearly——

GIL. I'll tell you what's happened. Something that should have happened twenty years ago. That's what's happened.

JULIE. Well, perhaps if—maybe—Gil, you'd better go now. I think you'd better go. It's late.

GIL. All right . . . Must I?

JULIE. Please.

GIL. I—I can't take you to the theatre?

JULIE. No—— *(Crosses left)* please. I must get Tony away on that boat—I couldn't give a performance if—just a minute alone——

GIL. It'll only be for a few hours—this time.

JULIE. You'll call for me at the theatre?

GIL. At eleven? Is that all right? *(Gets hat and coat.)*

JULIE. At eleven.

GIL. I'll be waiting.

JULIE. That'll be wonderful.

GIL. Good-bye.

(BUZZER.)

JULIE. *(Gayly)* Good-bye.

(GIL *goes.* JULIE *stands a moment. A step toward him as he departs. The buzzer off stage, right, sounds.* TONY *leaps out on balcony, clad in his*

B.V.D.'s and a bathrobe of silk worn open and billowing away behind him.)

TONY. *(Very loud)* Jo! Jo! Where's that bastard!

JULIE. Tony, be quiet! You'll wake mother!

TONY. Well, God damn it, I've got to get out! Jo!

(DELLA *enters, right, carrying a covered cup of hot soup on a small tray.)*

JULIE. Tony, will you shut up!

DELLA. Miss Julie, you'll have to be going. You've just got to have something hot in your stomach. Now, you drink this soup.

TONY. *(Simultaneous with* DELLA'S *speech above. Starting down the stairs, his robe ballooning behind him)* Della, where the hell is Jo? (Jo *enters, right, followed by* HALLBOY *in uniform.)* Jo, where the hell have you been? Come on! Bring that boy and come up here. I've got to get out!

JO. *(Crossing to a little flat-footed dog-trot)* Yes, sir. On the job. Got it all fixed. (JO *and* HALLBOY *go upstairs and exit in* TONY'S *room.)*

JULIE. *(Speaking on* DELLA'S *"You drink this soup")* What time is it? . . . Good heavens! . . . I can't stop to eat, Della . . . No, I can't! . . . Get my things . . . I've got to run . . . Look after mother, won't you? . . . Bring her some hot soup. . . . Tony, what's all this hullabaloo! Oh, if you were only out of this! *What* I wouldn't give for a little peace and quiet!

TONY. *(Toward stairs. Talks through last part of* JULIE'S *speech)* I'm not making any racket! You're making all the racket. Nobody'll be gladder than I am—— (FANNY *enters.)*

DELLA. *(Has placed tray on piano. Gets* JULIE'S

hat and coat. From the time of JULIE'S *refusal to take the soup she speaks on* JULIE'S *"only out of this.")* You know very well you can't give a performance on an empty stomach. Go fainting in the wings, and then what! You wouldn't even have to sit down to it. You could swallow this cup of good hot broth.

(As the three voices climax, speaking together, FANNY *appears on balcony from her room. She wears a rich and handsome dark silk dressing gown, voluminous and enveloping.)*

FANNY. Hush that clatter! Person can't get a wink!

JULIE. *(Goes toward her)* Mother! What are you doing up?

TONY. *(Is about to exit as he turns and sees* FANNY*—goes to her)* Hi there, Fanny! All right again! *(Pats her shoulder.)*

DELLA. Why, Mrs. Cavendish!

JULIE. Go back into your room this minute, Fanny Cavendish! Go back to bed!

*(*FANNY *starts down, assisted a step or two by* TONY, *who leaves her to* JULIE, *who has come up part way to meet her mother.* DELLA, *hat and coat in hand, remains* R.*)*

FANNY. What's going on here! What's the excitement!

TONY. There you are! You're the comeback kid!

JULIE. Mother, I wish you hadn't done this. I've got to go to the theatre . . . Gwen!

FANNY. I know. I know. Run along.

JULIE. I will not run along until you go back to bed. I want you to go back to bed.

FANNY. But I want to see Tony go! I can't stay in bed with Tony going!

JULIE. Tony, for heaven's sake, hurry up! How soon will you be ready?

TONY. All set! I'll be gone in thirty seconds. . . . All board for Europe! *(As* TONY *turns on balcony,* GWEN *comes out center door, balcony. She is still white and shaken. To* GWEN*)* Hello, there! (TONY *exits, center door.)*

GWEN. Mother, did you call me?

JULIE. Oh—yes, Gwen. I want you to look after mother. (GWEN *starts down stairs.* JULIE *is descending with* FANNY*)* I'm terribly late. Mother, lean on me. Gwen, take her other arm.

FANNY. I don't need any arm.

JULIE. Yes, but you do, though. You oughtn't to be up at all. Now Gwen's going to look after you—and Della, if you need me you're to telephone the box-office, you understand, and ask for Mr. Friedman—*you* know. I'll come right home after the performance—— No! Yes, I will! There! *(She has settled* FANNY *in her chair)* Now Della'll bring in your dinner, and Gwen'll get you anything you want, and oh, Gwen, you've been crying.

GWEN. No, I haven't.

DELLA. *(Still with* JULIE's *hat and coat)* Miss Julie, it's quarter to eight. You know what the traffic is.

JULIE. *(Has gone over to the piano on which the soup stands. Starts to drink a mouthful of it during this speech)* Oh, I've got to go through that crowd downstairs again! . . . Whew! this is hot! . . . And how Tony's ever going to manage it. . . . *(Calls)* Tony . . . are you ready?

TONY. *(Voice from balcony, off)* Right!

JULIE. I've got to know he's on that boat or I won't be able to play. . . . Mother, I want you to promise me to go back to bed the minute Tony's gone. Have your dinner in bed.

FANNY. Don't you fuss about me.

JULIE. But don't wait up for me, will you? Della, I can't take this. I'm not hungry. I haven't got time for it anyhow . . . *(Calls)* Tony! Are you coming? . . . *(To* DELLA*)* Hat! *(With a quick movement she seizes the hat from* DELLA'S *hand and pulls it down on her head.)*

TONY. *(Heard off)* All right! Go!

(Out of the balcony entrance and down the steps sweeps the cavalcade. It consists of JO *and* MAC, *laden with all the luggage that* TONY *arrived with on the preceding day. Then comes the* HALLBOY, *disguised in* TONY'S *hat and coat —the upturned fur collar, the pulled-down slouch hat, just as* TONY *entered in the first act. His face is concealed almost entirely by the coat collar and the hat.* JULIE *and* GWEN *follow the group on up into the alcove, shouting their good-byes and last-minute instructions.* FANNY *rises and stands about center, her arms out, as though expecting* TONY *to come to her before he goes out.)*

JULIE. The end of a perfect day. Thank God. Tony, don't charter a tug and come back—that's all I ask. Now, Jo, stay with him no matter what happens. (JO, MAC *and* HALLBOY *exit in hallway.* JULIE, GWEN *and* DELLA *follow off.)* How he's going to do it I don't know. I ought to go down with him.

GWEN. No, don't, mother!

FANNY. Good-bye, Tony! Good-bye, my boy!

JULIE. Take care of your sinus. Keep out of Russia. Why do you have to have golf clubs? *(From this point the voices of* FANNY, JULIE *and* GWEN *are heard simultaneously offstage.)* Don't start anything rough with anyone downstairs, for Heaven's sake! Jo, make him behave himself. Mac, I'm trusting you, too. They're sure to know him in those clothes. Why do you have to go to Europe! Well, anyhow, good-bye! Good-bye!

GWEN. Tony, take care of yourself. Send us a radio. Be sure! Be sure! I think it's absurd to take all that stuff. He could buy it all over there. Good-bye! Good-bye!

DELLA. *(Off)* Good-bye, Mr. Tony—good-bye.

FANNY. *(Standing at hall door)* Tony! Tony! Aren't you going to say good-bye!

(The three figures have swept down the stairs, been joined by DELLA, *have moved quickly across the room, and are now in the alcove on their way out.* JULIE, FANNY, *and* GWEN *stand aghast as they realize that* TONY *is not stopping to say good-bye.)*

JULIE. *(Off)* Tony, aren't you saying good-bye to us? He isn't saying good-bye.

GWEN. *(Off)* Tony! Wait a minute! Say good-bye to us all. Why, he isn't stopping! He's going! He's gone!

FANNY. Don't let him go! He's never gone like that! Come back and say good-bye! He didn't even talk to me! He didn't look at me! Tony! . . . Tony! . . . Tony! *(Growing weaker.* GWEN *goes to her.)*

JULIE. *(Rushing back to her)* Now, mother! He's all right! You wouldn't want him to stop! He'll send you a radio. Now don't! You'll only make yourself sick!

GWEN. Never mind, grandma—it'll be all right. I think it's a rotten shame.

JULIE. *(Darting toward the alcove, then realizing*

that her mother needs her more) Tony! Tony! . . . No, I guess I'd better not! *(Runs back to her mother)* Mother, you're all right, aren't you? Don't worry. I've got to go to the theatre!

(Through the outer door KITTY *and* DEAN *enter.* KITTY *leading.)*

KITTY. *(Off)* Why, the door's open.

DEAN. *(As he and* KITTY *enter)* What was that? Tony?

GWEN. Are you all right, Grandma?

JULIE. I wish I didn't have to go, Gwen. Do you think she's all right?

DEAN. What's the matter? Fanny sick?

KITTY. Listen, Julie Cavendish! I've got something to say to you.

JULIE. What?

(TONY, *in hallboy's uniform, darts out onto the balcony. He does not pause, but skims the balcony and down the stairs.)*

TONY. Hello, folks! Farewell appearance!

JULIE. *(In a sort of squawk that dies in her throat)* Oh! . . . Oh! . . . Oh, for . . .

FANNY. Tony!

GWEN. Oh!

DEAN. What *is* this?

KITTY. What's he doing?

TONY. *(Glances down at himself complacently)* How do you like it? Good on me? Isn't it?

JULIE. Tony! What are you going to do!

TONY. Going to the boat, of course.

FANNY. Like that!

TONY. Sure! They'll make a dash for their taxi—the crowd will all swarm after them—give 'em a nice run up Fifth Avenue. Then I go down, get into my cab, ten minutes I'm on the dock, voila!

DEAN. What's it all about?

FANNY. Tony, my boy!

TONY. *(A swift leap across the room)* Good-bye, everybody! *(Takes* FANNY'S *head in his two hands. Kisses her)* Good-bye, mother! *(A pose)* The open sea, the salt spray! The arctic wind! . . . I'm on my way! Remember it's the Guaranty Trust——

(Exit TONY, *outer door.* GWEN *sits on bench* R.*)*

FANNY. *(Rather feebly)* Tony! Tony! *(Sits on bench left of sofa.)*

DEAN. Why! What! . . . What!

JULIE. *(Who is standing near the sofa, sinks into it)* Ooooooh!

KITTY. *(Comes to* JULIE; *stands over her)* And now I want to ask you a question.

DEAN. Kitty!

KITTY. *(Sharply)* Did you offer me that part of your own accord, or did Bert put you up to it?

DEAN. Oh!

JULIE. *(From the position into which she slumped in the chair,* JULIE *begins to uncoil. Her eye is baleful. She rises slowly. Her whole attitude is so sinister and desperate that* KITTY *shrinks back a little)* No. No, it isn't possible! You! You come to me with your miserable little . . . Your part! Bert's . . . *(A little high hysterical laugh)* After all that I've . . . it's too . . . I can't . . .

GWEN. Mother! Don't! (PERRY *enters.)* Perry!

PERRY. What's the matter? What's going on?

JULIE. Well—what else? What else? Come on! What else? Perry! for God's sake take her out of this! Take her away before it's too late. Take her where she'll never hear stage again! Take her away!

FANNY. Julie! Julie!

GWEN. No! I'm not going to marry him!

(A Warning.)

JULIE. *(Pushes her hair back from her forehead with her open palm—a gesture of desperation)* Not going to marry him! Not going—— *(A finger pointing to the spot where* JULIE, GWEN *and* FANNY *have talked earlier.)*

GWEN. I'm not going to marry him and spoil his life!

PERRY. Gwen!

GWEN. No, no!

JULIE. Oh, no, you won't! If you think I'm going to let you throw away your whole life! . . . And for what? . . . *This!* . . . . So that nineteen years from now you can be standing here as I am, a mad woman in a family of maniacs! Money for this one, jobs for that one, rehearsals and readings and tickets for God knows where. I'm damned if you're going to! You're going to marry Perry Stewart——

GWEN. No, no!

JULIE. Oh, yes, you are! You're going to do what I didn't do. They told me I had to be a Cavendish. *(A movement from her mother.)* Oh, yes, you did! *(Wheeling to* GWEN *again)* Well, you're not going to be one. You're going to marry him now—to-night—to-morrow. And I'm going to be there with you, and stand up beside you, and cry for happiness, and wish to God it was me! *(Her voice suddenly low, thoughtful)* And why not? I'm not dead yet. I've got some of my life left. And I'm going to live it to suit *me!* You've all had your turn. Who's crazy *now!* I can walk out and nobody can stop me.

FANNY. What nonsense!

DEAN. You're mad!

JULIE. You don't believe it, h'm? I'll show you. I'm going to marry Gil Marshall and go to Egypt and Venice and Constantinople—and what do you know about that? As far as the stage is concerned—

I'm through with it. Cavendish! To hell with Cavendish! I'm never going to act again. I'm never going to set foot on another stage as long as I live. I'm never going inside a theatre! I'm ne——

JO. *(Aghast at finding* JULIE *still at home, has heard her voice, high-pitched. In a voice of alarm)* Miss Julie! It's eight o'clock!

JULIE. *(Grabs her coat from* JO. *Rushes in a panic toward the outer door)* Oh, my God!

CURTAIN

ACT III

The scene is the same. The time, a year later. November. As always, flowers are everywhere. The small table upstage, left of the stairs, is decked with a rich lace tea cloth. The table and armchair have been restored to their former position—left of the sofa. The door at right is open; so are the doors to the library.

At the rise DELLA *enters from right. She is carrying a silver tea service—gleaming with cups and silver pitchers. She puts it down on the lace-covered table; starts to arrange the cups.* JULIE *strolls casually out onto the balcony, from her room. She wears a costume slip of gold or silver, with only straps over the shoulder. Obviously a tea coat is presently to be slipped over this. She is polishing her nails with a buffer. She throws a careless glance toward* FANNY'S *room; her gaze takes in the room below.*

JULIE. Oh, Della.

DELLA. Yes, Miss Julie.

JULIE. Let's have tea in the library. I think it'd be cozier.

DELLA. All right. *(Starts to pile up the cups again.)*

FANNY. *(Her voice through the open door of her room)* What's that smells so good?

JULIE. *(Sniffs)* Gingerbread, I guess, for tea.

(JO *enters at right, carrying a little stack of plates.)*

DELLA. Library, Jo.

JO. *(Crossing to tea tray)* Oh . . . How many there going to be?

DELLA. Half a dozen, she said. Better count on twelve.

(JULIE *on balcony, putting some last touches to the adjustment of her costume.)*

JULIE. Jo, did you start a fire in the library?

JO. Yes, Miss Julie. Nice bright one. *(Exits into library.)*

DELLA. I told him to build one soon's I heard Miss Gwen was bringing the baby over.

JULIE. *(Coming down stairs)* Coming down, mother?

FANNY. *(From her room)* Minute.

JULIE. *(Descending)* Got on your plum silk?

FANNY. Yes, *sir!*

DELLA. *(Indicating a vase of roses)* I brought Mr. Marshall's roses out into this room. I thought you'd want 'em where he'd be sure to see them.

JULIE. Thanks, Della.

DELLA. Wonder what Mr. Marshall will say to Miss Gwen's baby. He knows about him, doesn't he?

JULIE. I wrote him, Della—let's hope he approves. *(Sits on sofa. Gathers up a few letters from the table.* Jo *enters and crosses.)* You might shake up a few cocktails, Jo. Somebody'll want them.

JO. Right. *(Exits right.)*

DELLA. He'd better approve. *(Crosses right)* I never saw a grander baby in all my life. Two months old, and you'd think he was twice that.

JULIE. *(Absorbed in a letter. Absently)* You must tell that to Miss Gwen.

DELLA. I bet he don't see babies like that down

in South America. Anyhow, they're black, ain't they?

JULIE. M-m—well, maybe cafe au lait.

DELLA. *(A moment's hesitation. Then, with determination to know)* Miss Julie, are you going to live down there in South America when you marry Mr. Marshall?

JULIE. *(Looks up)* Mr. Marshall doesn't live there, Della.

DELLA. Well, he's been there twice this year, and this last time about six months. That's living there, ain't it?

JULIE. Oh, he won't be there much, next year. *(Again turns her attention to her mail.)*

DELLA. You see, I'm only asking you on account— Excuse me, Miss Julie, but I don't know if you're going to give up the apartment or what. You see, with Miss Gwen with her own place now, and you going to get married and go traveling——

JULIE. Well, I wouldn't worry about that, Della. We may not give up the apartment after all.

DELLA. But who's going to live in it? With Mrs. Cavendish going touring on the road——

JULIE. I don't know about that, Della. The doctor doesn't think she ought to go on the road.

DELLA. But she was only telling me five minutes ago——

JULIE. Yes—yes, I know. But mother is not going to be able to travel again, Della.

DELLA. What? *(*JULIE *turns and looks at* DELLA*)* Oh, my God! *(*FANNY *is heard coming.)*

JULIE. Be quiet!

*(*FANNY *enters from her room onto balcony. She wears the plum silk gown, very proud. Her cane has been discarded. Her step is quick and firm. She descends the stairs.)*

FANNY. "And purple her habiliments and scarlet was her soul. Romeo, wherefore art thou, Romeo?" Well, where's your young man? You'd think he'd come bounding right up from the dock after being away so long. (DELLA *exits, right.)*

JULIE. He'll be along presently. He phoned from the hotel.

FANNY. Well, if he said he'd come, he'll come. He's what they call steady-going. Regular habits. Look at those two dozen American beauties—*(A gesture in their direction)*—that have been arriving every morning, like the milk.

JULIE. I think it was very sweet of him to leave an order like that.

FANNY. If there's one way to take the romance out of roses, it's knowing that you're going to get them every day.

JULIE. But the very qualities he's got are the ones I need. I've had enough of temperamental people.

FANNY. I'll bet he's worked out your honeymoon in algebra. Arrive Constantinople January twelfth, arrive Cairo February twenty-fourth. He'll tell you that the next Sahara sunset is at 6:49, and it had better be. And while you're sitting on the hill at Fiesole he'll know to the minute when you'll be in Copenhagen.

JULIE. Even that'll be restful. After twenty years of practically checking my own trunk.

FANNY. If you wanted to marry him, why didn't you do it a year ago? Why didn't you marry him then?

JULIE. You know why I didn't. There was Wolfe with a new theatre all built—a new production on his hands—and then Gwen dropping out of it. I had to agree to play the New York run. How'd I know it was going to be a whole year!

FANNY. Where're you going on your wedding trip? Made up your mind yet?

JULIE. Why, I don't know. It'll depend on what Gil says, a good deal. I'm not keen about these far-away places.

FANNY. Since when! Why, it's been Bagdad and Venice and the Vale of Kashmir every day of the past year!

JULIE. Well, I love the sound of the names, but they are awfully far away.

FANNY. If you're going to marry him at all, you might as well see the world. You'll need it.

JULIE. I just thought I'd like to be around in case you needed me—you or Gwen.

FANNY. What for? Gwen certainly doesn't need you. Settled and through with the stage.

JULIE. Yes . . . still . . .

FANNY. And as for me, while you're drifting down the Nile I'll be playing Ogden, Utah, and doing pretty well. I sold out there in 1924.

JULIE. Now look here, mother. I've been thinking it over—your going on this tour—and I'd ever so much rather you wouldn't go.

FANNY. What!

JULIE. You haven't been well. I wouldn't have any peace if I had to think of you galloping around those terrible towns—Tulsa, Albuquerque, Oklahoma City. I know I couldn't stand a tour like that.

FANNY. I'm tougher than you are. When I quit it'll be for the same reason that Aubrey did. And no other.

JULIE. Well, I don't think you ought to go. Besides, there's Gwen. She's awfully young. . . . I'd feel so much better if you were here to look after her.

FANNY. What's the matter with her husband?

JULIE. Besides, there's this place—— Della was just asking if you were going to give it up—— And then there's Bert——

(DOOR Bell.)

FANNY. And Kitty. *(Outer door bell rings.)*

JULIE. You see, if you stay here, all comfortable, it'll mean I'll have some place to come back to when I'm in New York.

FANNY. Oh! So as to make you comfortable I'm to give up my whole career!

JULIE. No, no. It isn't me. It's you. You must admit it's a hard trip, and——

(JO *enters right, goes toward outer door.)*

FANNY. *(Rising slowly)* This'll be your Emerald King.

JULIE. I suppose so.

DEAN. *(His voice heard off as* JO *opens the door)* Good afternoon.

JO. Afternoon, Mr. Dean.

FANNY. It's Bert.

JULIE. Oh, mother!

(BERT *and* KITTY *enter from the alcove, followed by* JO. *During the next few speeches* JO *takes their coats and* DEAN'S *hat; hangs them in alcove closet.* KITTY *is dressed with some expensiveness—perhaps a fur coat.* DEAN, *who has been quite gray and nearly bald in the preceding acts, displays, when he removes his hat, a fine and unexpected crop of coal black hair.)*

KITTY. Isn't it a marvelous day?

DEAN. Ah! Here we are!

FANNY. Hello, there, Bertie. Kitty.

JULIE. *(Weakly)* Why, hello.

DEAN. Just thought we'd drop in and see how you all were.

KITTY. Mm, what a smart tea coat, Julie!

JULIE. Do you like it?

KITTY. Oh, yes. I think the color's a little trying.

DEAN. Thanks, Jo. *(As he helps him with his coat. He is up near alcove)* Marshall's boat get in? I see he's due.

JULIE. Yes, it did. He'll be here very soon.

KITTY. Oh, won't that be nice? We'll be here to greet him. *(Sits on sofa.)*

JULIE. Tha-t's—lovely.

DEAN. *(Crossing left)* Queer fellow, Marshall. Always talking about the Panama Canal. . . . Well, Fanny, still determined to go out into the hinterland?

FANNY. Why not?

DEAN. No reason. Just be careful, that's all. You're not as young as you were, you know.

FANNY. Who is?

KITTY. Won't be many more chances for family gatherings, will there, Mother Cavendish? (DELLA *enters and exits library with tray with cake, etc. A bitter look of resentment from* FANNY.) You won't be keeping this great big place when the family breaks up. (DELLA *enters with tray containing cake —pitcher of hot water for tea. She crosses left.)*

FANNY. I was not aware that the Cavendish family is breaking up. *(Rises.* JO *enters from hallway and exits under stairs.)*

KITTY. Well, after all, with you on the road, and Julie God knows where, and Gwen married—I don't see that you'll have any use for it. You can't count on Tony. It looks as if he's going to stay in Europe forever.

DEAN. *(Intercepting* DELLA *as she passes him with her laden tray, gathers up a rich and crumbly piece of cake, which he negotiates with some difficulty through the following lines)* Just what are your plans, Fanny? *(Pauses, cake in hand, ready for a bite)* How about all this stuff? *(A huge bite)* What are you going to do with everything? *(A gesture that indicates the room about him, but which does not disturb the precarious business in hand.)*

(DELLA *exits, library.)*

FANNY. *(Crosses up)* It'll all go to the storehouse, I suppose. And Aubrey there along with it. . . . But we're held together by something more than tables and chairs. *(Comes down.)*

KITTY. It occurred to me this morning—remember I was saying to you, Bert—that aside from Fanny on the road, it will be Bert and I who'll be carrying on the family tradition.

FANNY. Thanks for including me, anyhow.

KITTY. Has Bert told you what we're planning to do?

FANNY. Why, no.

JULIE. No.

DEAN. *(All eyes on him)* Well, I was keeping it as a sort of surprise.

JULIE. Why, Bert, what is it?

FANNY. What are you going to do?

BERT. Why, it seems that the vaudeville people are very anxious to elevate the tone of their entertainments.

FANNY. Vaudeville?

DEAN. Why not? Why not? They don't want good plays any more. They proved that in the way they received "The Conqueror." Finest play of my career, and what happened?

FANNY. It closed. *(Sits.)*

DEAN. Now, here comes this opportunity to reach a wide public, to create an audience for the finer things.

KITTY. We're getting eighteen hundred dollars a week, together.

DEAN. Ah—yes, and twenty weeks right in New York, and around it. They've got up a very neat little act for us. Amusing. Human. Now, here's the plot——

JULIE. Oh, yes, tell us.

FANNY. I'm all a-twitter.

DEAN. I'm a sort of a bachelor chap—thirty-five or thereabouts—very rich, and have had an unhappy love affair that I tell the butler about.

KITTY. Ever since then you've been a woman hater.

DEAN. Yes, yes.

KITTY. Yes, yes.

DEAN. Then comes this letter from Australia. It seems that an old college friend has died out there, and it was his last wish that I should take care of his little girl—be her guardian.

JULIE. The letter is delayed in transit, so that it happens to arrive just before the little girl herself.

DEAN. You've read it.

JULIE. Oh, no. No.

DEAN. All events, presently there's a lot of noise outside—automobile horn, so on—the door's opened, and instead of the little child they were expecting, there stands an exquisite young girl of eighteen.

FANNY. Kitty. (FANNY, *without a word, rises and starts for the library.)*

(DOOR Bell.)

DEAN. Hold on, Fanny—I'm not through.

FANNY. *(Going left)* Oh, yes, you are. Besides, that's probably Marshall. Why don't you two come in here with me for a while?

(DELLA *enters from library. Goes toward front door.)*

DELLA. Tea's all ready, Mrs. Cavendish. *(Crosses and exits under stairs.* JO *enters and goes to door.)*

FANNY. Come on. Have some tea. *(A step or*

two toward library door. A feeling of general movement of the group, left.)

KITTY. I come in with my little dog Rags, that my father gave me—*(As she talks she is walking toward left in what evidently is meant to be the way in which* BERT'S *ward will walk)*—and I'm sort of a pathetic figure.

FANNY. You don't say!

WOLFE. *(Heard as* JO *opens the door)* Well, Jo! The whole family here?

DEAN. *(At the sound of his voice) Ah!*

KITTY. Well!

JULIE. Ah, Oscar.

WOLFE. *(Entering. To* JULIE) Don't Oscar me, you renegade! *(Gives* JO *hat and coat, who takes them in hallway.)* Hello, folks! Fanny, my girl! *(Turns again to* JULIE) A lot you care about Oscar. All you're thinking about is this Whozis. The boat gets in to-day, huh? It couldn't sink or anything?

JULIE. Your own fault, Oscar. Why didn't you marry me?

WOLFE. *(Cross on speech)* Say, it's bad enough to manage you. . . . Well, Fanny, how are you? Good as ever?

FANNY. Certainly am. Come on—I want my tea.

WOLFE. Don't you go back on me like these other loafers. With Julie a millionaire's bride, and Gwen a society matron, all I need is you should marry John D. Rockefeller and my season is over.

FANNY. About time you had to concentrate on me. I want a brand new play for next season, and none of your cold storage tidbits.

WOLFE. *(To* JULIE) You hear that? There's a trouper for you!

JULIE. Anyhow, Oscar, I was a good fellow when I had it.

DEAN. And I'll come back to you, old fellow. This little flyer in vaudeville.

WOLFE. Mm . . . Oh, Fanny! I knew there was something. Can you open a week earlier, do you think? Toledo on the 14th—all right with you?

FANNY. *(Doubtfully)* Full week in Toledo?

WOLFE. Well, maybe we should split it with Columbus, huh? Toledo ain't so good this year.

FANNY. *(With asperity)* I can play the full week. *(Turns to exit.)*

KITTY. *(Following her as all drift toward library doors)* Now I want to tell you about my part. Did we tell you it's called "The Bachelor's Baby"? Well, of course, my part is really just as important as Bert's——

(FANNY, KITTY *and* BERT *exit into library.* WOLFE *is about to follow.)*

JULIE. Oscar, Oscar!

WOLFE. Huh?

JULIE. Wait a minute. (JULIE *quietly closes the library doors.)*

WOLFE. What's going on?

JULIE. I've got to talk to you. *(She stands listening a brief moment to make sure that the others cannot hear.)*

WOLFE. What's the matter?

JULIE. It's about Fanny.

WOLFE. Yeh? What's up?

JULIE. *(Pause)* Oscar, she can't go on this tour.

WOLFE. Why not?

JULIE. I don't know how you're going to do it, but some way or other you've got to keep her from going. Without her knowing it.

WOLFE. *(His keen gaze on her)* What are you trying to tell me, Julie?

JULIE. I went to see Randall yesterday.

WOLFE. Yes?

JULIE. She's through, Oscar.

WOLFE. *(Dully)* What!

JULIE. She can't go on this tour. She can't do anything.

WOLFE. What do you mean?

JULIE. She's got to have absolute quiet and rest. The least strain or exertion, and she's likely to go —like that.

WOLFE. . . . Fanny?

JULIE. *(Crosses right)* She never can play again —anywhere. She may never even leave this house.

WOLFE. Let me—let me realize this. Fanny Cavendish—in there—it's all over? (JULIE *nods.)* I don't know why I'm so—after all, she's been sick now a long time; she ain't young any more—but she never seemed sick—always going on again—busy with plans—sweeping us all along—it don't seem possible that——

(JULIE'S *warning hand halts* WOLFE'S *speech.* FANNY *appears in library doorway.)*

FANNY. Della! Della! No more mind than a rabbit.

WOLFE. *(Elaborately casual)* So I says to him, that's one way of looking at it. Everybody's got his own ideas——

JULIE. I think you're quite right, Oscar. I thought of that myself.

FANNY. Don't you two ever talk anything but business! . . . Della! (DELLA *appears, right.)*

DELLA. Yes, Mrs. Cavendish.

FANNY Where's that gingerbread?

DELLA. We tried to cut it and it crumbled.

FANNY. Bring it in anyhow. (DELLA *goes.)* Don't you two want your tea?

JULIE. Right away, mother.

FANNY. Kitty's reached the love interest. *(Draws her skirts and very coquettishly exits in library.)*

JULIE. *(Talking for* FANNY'S *benefit as she goes quietly up to close library door)* Of course, Oscar, in one way I agree with you, but, on the other hand, I don't think it wise—— *(Closes door. Turns to* OSCAR) What are we going to tell her, Oscar? How are we going to manage it?

WOLFE. I tell you how I fix it. First I tell her on account of booking troubles we can't open just yet—make it March, say, instead of January. Then when March comes along, it's late in the season, the road ain't so good any more—maybe we ought to wait till next year. And I guarantee you, the way I do it, she won't suspect a thing.

JULIE. Oscar, what a grand person you are.

WOLFE. I wish I could really do something. Thirty-five years we been together. They don't make them like her any more . . . I wish you could have seen her the first time I did, Julie. Her face. Young, and gay, and beautiful—but so much more than beautiful. And how she treated me that first meeting. Me—a beginner, a nobody. I went into there, I tried not to show how I was shaking. I came out, I could have been Sir Charles Wyndham.

JULIE. Oscar, if I could only tell you what you've meant to all of us! But you wouldn't listen.

WOLFE. And—you, Julie?

JULIE. What?

WOLFE. What about your plans, with this news? Still Egypt and India?

JULIE. Oh, no. But—what am I going to do, Oscar? Gil's got his heart set on the ends of the earth—he hates New York; I don't dare go far away.

WOLFE. Well, say. You tell him how things stand, what the situation is. After all, he can't be quite a—I mean, in the face of something like this, surely now——

JULIE. Oscar, why don't you like Gil? I wish you did.

WOLFE. Marshall? I like him all right. He ain't just my kind, but maybe I ain't his, either.

JULIE. Oscar, do you think if I asked him he'd be willing to take a house here in town for a while? Then I could look after her—be here if—anything happened.

WOLFE. How could he say no—a time like this?

JULIE. I'd feel so relieved.

WOLFE. Only what would you do with yourself all the time? New York—you've seen New York. Running a house—what's that for you? What are you going to do?

JULIE. Why, I don't know. It's all so sudden—I hadn't thought about it yet.

WOLFE. Well, then, say! You're living in New York anyhow; you haven't got anything to do; what's the difference if——

JULIE. No, no! I'm through with it, Oscar. Through with it forever.

WOLFE. So. You—Gwen—Fanny—that ends it, huh? And for you there's no excuse.

JULIE. I'm going to be married, Oscar. That's a pretty good excuse.

WOLFE. Tell me, what do you talk about when you're alone with this fellow? The theatre he says he don't care about. Imagine!

JULIE. There are other things in the world beside the theatre.

WOLFE. Sure! But not for you.

JULIE. I want to relax, and play around, and have some fun.

WOLFE. Fun! Fun is work! It's work that's fun. You've had more fun in the last twenty years than any woman in America. And let me tell you, Julie, the theatre is just beginning in this country. It used to be London—Paris—Berlin. Now it's New York.

I tell you, a fine actress to-day—there's nothing she can't do. And the finest one of them all, that could do the biggest things of them all, *she* says she wants to have fun.

JULIE. Oh, Oscar, there are lots of actresses, and so many good ones. *(Cross right.)*

WOLFE. Yes, good, but not for this play.

JULIE. What play?

WOLFE. Not even any of these young ones that are coming up. Gwen maybe. A little young, but she could do it. Only—*(A gesture of helplessness)*—she's gone, too.

JULIE. Oscar, what play? What are you talking about?

WOLFE. Julie, I've never been one of these artistic producers—*you* know—The Theatre of The Future. Way back when I was a call boy at Daly's Theatre for two dollars a week I made up my mind show business was a good place to make money in, and so I went into it, and I been in it forty years, and I haven't got a nickel. Mind you, I've done a few good plays, too, but always I had an idea they would also make a few dollars. But this time it's different. I have got, I tell you, a play I am so crazy to produce it I don't care how much I lose on it.

JULIE. Really, Oscar! What is it? Who wrote it!

WOLFE. A new fellow you never heard of. Gunther his name is—a college professor out in Idaho. You wouldn't believe a college professor could know so much. He sits out there in that desert, mind you, and he writes this play and he doesn't know himself how good it is.

JULIE. What's it about?

WOLFE. That doesn't matter—it's how he does it. It's going to bring in a whole new kind of playwriting. They've never seen anything like this! God, what a play!

JULIE. Oscar! How exciting!

WOLFE. Exciting, yes. If I can do it right. But how am I going to do it. You gone. Gwen gone.

JULIE. You'll find some one. You're sure to.

WOLFE. All right. Never mind. Go ahead and relax—relax, when you could be making history. I do the play anyhow. Not so perfect maybe—but I do it. I do it because I want to be known as the man who produced this play.

JULIE. But if it's as good as that it would run years and years, wouldn't it?

WOLFE. No. A month—two months—I don't give it more than that. The first one's like this—they got to get used to them.

JULIE. I couldn't, Oscar. I couldn't.

WOLFE. All right. Get married and be a bazaar patroness. Mark my words, you'll come back again.

JULIE. They don't always come back. Look at Gwen. And Tony! He's been away a year.

(The sound of the opening of the outer door, and a gay call from GWEN.*)*

GWEN. *(Off)* Yoo-hoo!

JULIE. Gwen! *(Meets* GWEN *up right.* GWEN *and* PERRY *enter.)*

GWEN. *(Greets* JULIE*)* Oh, how nice! Hello there! *(Crosses to* OSCAR.*)*

WOLFE. Hello, children! And how's the mama?

JULIE. *(Greets* PERRY. *A line shot through the greetings)* Where's the baby?

PERRY. Hello, everybody!

*(*OSCAR *crosses, shakes hands with* PERRY *and then goes down right. Attracted by the sound of* GWEN'S *voice,* FANNY, *followed by* DEAN *and* KITTY, *enter from library.* DEAN *pops a final bite of cake into his mouth. Dusts his hands briskly.)*

FANNY. So it is . . . Hello, there . . . and Perry.

DEAN. How are you! How are you!

KITTY. Hello! Hardly ever see you people.

GWEN. *(Crossing to* FANNY*)* How are you, Grandma, dear? You look wonderful. . . . Hello, Kitty!

(PERRY, *a little aloof from the others, nods his greetings, or conveys it with a little wave of the hand.)*

FANNY. I'm fine. How's Aubrey?

KITTY. Where is he? Where's the baby?

JULIE. Don't tell me he isn't coming? (PERRY *crosses to piano.)*

GWEN. Oh, yes, Miss Peake's bringing him. She makes him rest two minutes before his bottle or three minutes after—I never can remember. We didn't wait. . . . Where's Gil? I thought he'd be here.

(PERRY, *still with an air of detachment from the group, is up at the piano, leaning over it, his back partly turned to the others. He is glancing idly at the pages of a book, without seeming really to be interested in it.* FANNY *is sitting in chair left of sofa.)*

JULIE. He'll be here soon.

GWEN. Oh, fine!

WOLFE. Soon enough he'll be here. All the way from South America he's got to come to ruin my business. And Perry here—he couldn't pick out a nice girl from Park Avenue some place. It's got to be a Cavendish. Huh?

PERRY. How's that? *(Emerges briefly from his book.)*

WOLFE. I say, you couldn't marry a good Junior League actress, huh? Instead of my Gwen.

PERRY. Oh . . . uh . . . yeh.

GWEN. Now, Perry!

JULIE. The boy friend's a little upstage to-day, isn't he?

GWEN. No, he isn't. Are you, Perry?

PERRY. I didn't think I was. Gosh, I want to do whatever . . . *(Comes down, slowly)* Why don't you tell *them* about it? See what they think. *(Crosses up to secretary.)*

JULIE. Why, what's up? *(Cross to sofa, sits.* KITTY *goes back of sofa.)*

FANNY. What is it?

GWEN. Well—it's me. *(Sits on sofa.)* Now, this is the way it is. The baby's two months old, and he's the darlingest baby that ever lived, but he doesn't do anything but sleep all the time, and, according to Miss Peake's schedule, you can only play with him about four minutes a day. Of course, when he gets older, it'll be different, but just now he doesn't need me at all. I'm in the way!

PERRY. How can you be in the way! *(Comes down.)*

GWEN. I am in the way. *(Turns to the others.)* She glares whenever I pick him up. I thought there'd be all kinds of things to do for him, but there aren't. So here I am with absolutely nothing to do until he gets so he kind of knows me. And on top of that, here's Perry going away on a business trip. He'll be gone about four weeks, anyway.

PERRY. I may be back in three.

GWEN. The whole thing's only five. . . . Now, this is what's happened.

JULIE. Well, thank God.

GWEN. They've got this Hungarian play and hey've offered me a simply marvelous part——

JULIE. Who has?

GWEN. The Theatre Guild.
FANNY. Theatre Guild!
DEAN. What? What?
GWEN. It only means every other week, because they're going to alternate with Shaw's play.
FANNY. You're going on again!
GWEN. No. It's only for the subscription period, unless it turns out to be a great hit, and this can't.
KITTY. Well!

(On JULIE'S *face there is a look which is not altogether happy. There is something of shock in* GWEN'S *news, and, for her, something of apprehension. Somehow, this makes* JULIE'S *leaving the stage a little less agreeable.)*

WOLFE. Hold on a minute. Let me understand this. You're going back on the stage? Is that it?
GWEN. *(Cross to* OSCAR) No. Nothing like that. It's only for these few weeks, and just because it's a marvelous part. She's a slavey in this Budapest household—the kind of thing I've always been crazy to play—apron and cotton stockings and my hair pulled back tight. . . . Oh, Perry, it would be such fun!
KITTY. Well, this is *news!*
FANNY. And about time!
DEAN. Nice little organization—the Theatre Guild.
PERRY. Gosh, Gwen! I don't mind a few weeks if it's going to make you as happy as that.
GWEN. Oh, Perry! *(Throws her arms about him. Kisses him.)* Isn't he a darling!
KITTY. It's really thrilling, to think of Gwen going back. Aren't you thrilled, Julie?
JULIE. Why—I should say—I am! *(Rises, goes to* GWEN) Gwen, darling, I'm very happy— *(Then goes up.)*
GWEN. I'm as excited as if I'd never been on

the stage before! My, it'll be funny to see my picture in the papers again. To tell the truth, I've sort of missed it.

FANNY. How soon are you going to open?

GWEN. About a month, I guess. We go into rehearsal next week.

DEAN. That'll be a first night!

KITTY. I should say so.

(DOOR Bell.)

GWEN. It's really a terrific part. She carries the whole play. I'm scared pink, but of course if I can do it it'll put me where I can—it'll be dandy! *(A little embarrassed laugh. The outer door bell rings.)*

JULIE. Yes. Won't it!

WOLFE. Five weeks, eh? *(Thoughtfully)* That means you are through with it early in February.

GWEN. *(Puzzled)* What? (WOLFE *pats* GWEN'S *hand and chuckles with delight.)*

(DELLA *enters, right, goes to answer door.* JO *follows almost immediately, right, carrying tray of cocktail shaker and glasses.)*

DEAN. Ah! (JO *puts tray on table, left.)*

GWEN. Perry, you do feel all right about it, don't you? Because if you don't, I just won't do it, that's all.

PERRY. Well, of course you'll do it. What do a few weeks matter!

(They cross to bench in front of window. DEAN *strolls up toward the cocktails.* JO, *at his approach, begins to shake them, genially. He pours one for* DEAN.)

DELLA. *(At door, off)* Welcome back, Mr. Marshall.

GIL. *(Also heard off)* Thank you. Della. How are you?

JULIE. It's Gil.

(GIL *enters from the alcove. He pauses a moment on the threshold. Seeing that others are present, he contents himself with kissing* JULIE'S *hand. Then he greets the others. The following lines are said in unison)*

FANNY. Well, at last!

DEAN. Ah, Marshall!

GWEN. It's Gil!

KITTY. Well—well——

GIL. Julie, dear!

JULIE. Gil!

GIL. It's good to see you—to be back.

(There is a general handshaking—greeting—business of welcome, with, perhaps, two shaking his hands at the same time.)

DEAN. Hello, there, old fellow.

KITTY. Welcome back, Mr. Marshall.

GWEN. Hello, there. How brown you are!

(GIL *shakes hands with* GWEN *and* PERRY.)

GIL. Think so? And how's the little mother?

PERRY. Hello, Marshall. Glad to see you.

WOLFE. Mr. Marshall.

GIL. *(To* WOLFE) How do you do? *(To* FANNY, *goes* C.*)* How well you're looking.

FANNY. Never was better. How are you, Gil?

GIL. Fine, thanks—— *(To* KITTY) And how are you?

KITTY. Fine. (DELLA *exits right.)*

GIL. Well! It's nice to find you all gathered here

like this. I'm going to assume it's all in my honor, too.

KITTY. Indeed, yes!

DEAN. Cocktail, Marshall? *(Offers glass.)*

GIL. Uh—no, I don't believe I will. I'm used to a different kind of stuff, down there. I'm a little afraid of the New York brand.

FANNY. I'll take one, Bertie.

(DEAN *hands* FANNY *a cocktail, then gets one for himself.* JO *takes off silver service in library.)*

JULIE. How was the trip, Gil? How many knots an hour, and all that sort of thing? *(Sits on sofa.)*

GIL. *(Stands center)* Oh, about as usual. Pretty hot when we started, but cooled off when we came up north.

DEAN. *(Down left)* How long does that trip take, anyhow? Three weeks, isn't it? (OSCAR *crosses up and sits on chair* R.)

GIL. Eighteen and a half days, as a rule, with fair weather. Let me see—yes, we made it in eighteen and a half days, this time.

GWEN. Oh, what a trip! I'd be bored to death, wouldn't you? *(To* JULIE.)

JULIE. Why—I don't know. No. The boat might be full of dashing young Brazilians, or one or two of the Horsemen of the Apocalypse——

GIL. As a matter of fact, there was a very representative crowd on board this trip. Some of the biggest planters in South America. Zamaco. Manolo Berlanga.

FANNY. Really?

GIL. *(A sudden recollection)* Oh, here's something that'll interest you folks. *(Crosses left.)* There was a theatrical troupe on board. American. They'd been down in Buenos Aires trying to play in English. Ridiculous, of course! Poor devils! Didn't even have money enough to pay their passage. There they all were, on the dock. Of course we couldn't see them stranded. So we got together enough to see them home. I guess I felt a little sentimental about them on account of you people.

JULIE. Oh! *(A second's rather terrible pause.)*

FANNY. Really!

GIL. Seems the manager skipped out with the money. You know the way those fellows are. *(Crosses to center.)* Think they'd be down-hearted, but they were carefree enough, once they got on the boat. Turned out to be a very decent lot. *(Sits on sofa.)* Couple of them were married—uh—lived in Jersey some place—had—uh—— (JO *has entered during this speech.)*

(This speech of GIL'S *has been received with a mannerly but stony silence on the part of the* CAVENDISH *family.)*

FANNY. I'll go in and finish my tea. *(To* JULIE *and* GIL.*)* . . . Jo, some hot water. Put a log on the fire.

(She goes toward library as she speaks. Exits library. JO *exits right.* GIL *and* PERRY *rise.* DEAN *and* KITTY *exit in* FANNY'S *wake.)*

GWEN. *(Rather breathlessly)* Is it true that it's winter in South America when it's summer in New York?

GIL. Yes. The seasons are just the opposite from yours.

GWEN. How funny! *(Crossing to left)* But then I suppose they think *we're* funny.

GIL. No. You see, they travel a great deal—understand how it is.

GWEN. Oh. *(Indicates to* PERRY *to come along.)*

GIL. Well! And so you've got a family now, h'm? How is she? Am I going to see her?

PERRY. She's a boy. *(Crossing left to* GWEN.)

GIL. Well, that *was* a boner, wasn't it! Anyhow, I imagine you're the busy little wife and mother nowadays. No more of this theatrical business, h'm?

GWEN. Well——

JULIE. Gwen is going into a new play. *(Rise, goes right.)*

PERRY. Yes.

GIL. A new play! Why, how old is your child!

GWEN. Not old enough to miss me—is he, Perry? . . . Come on, let's have some tea.

(GWEN *exits into library.* PERRY *looks at* GIL. *There is a foolish little grin on his face. Exits after* GWEN.)

WOLFE. I hope to see you again, Mr. Gilbert Marshall. *(Exits library.)*

(The door closes part way as he draws it behind him on leaving. GIL *acknowledges this with a little formal nod. He waits for the library door to close partly. Turns eagerly to her.)*

GIL. Julie! Julie! How I've missed you! *(Goes to her.)*

JULIE. Gil! How could you!

GIL. What!

JULIE. How could you talk like that! Didn't you see how they—— Oh, Gil!

GIL. What do you mean? What did I do!

JULIE. You—— Oh, never mind. It doesn't matter.

GIL. But Julie, if you'd just tell me. What was it!

JULIE. No. . . . Tell me about your . . . trip,

Gil. Did you have a nice time? *(Crosses to sofa—sits.)*

GIL. The trip didn't matter. It just meant reaching you. You're looking just lovely, Julie. I've never seen you so beautiful. *(She turns a cheek to him, coldly. There is nothing else she can do.)* It's been the longest six months of my life. When you finally wired that the end was in sight—that the play was actually closing—do you know what I did? I gave everybody on the place a holiday with double pay.

JULIE. I'm very—honored.

GIL. *(Sits on arm of sofa, right)* They're like a lot of children, down there. It's a great country, Julie.

JULIE. It must be.

GIL. It's as different from the life up here as you can imagine. You'll love it. At Cordoba I was in bed every night at ten o'clock, for four months. Up at six, in the saddle eight hours a day.

JULIE. Oh! Yes?

GIL. Julie. It's so beautiful—and peaceful—and big! And you'll meet real people. None of your . . . Solid! Substantial! The kind that make a country what it is. This man Zamaco who was on the boat. He's my nearest neighbor, you know. Has the next estancia.

JULIE. Oh, yes. You told me.

GIL. Yes, indeed. You'll see a lot of the Zamacos. He's a Spaniard of the highest type—very big cattle man. She was a Kansas City girl—Krantz—you know—daughter of Julius Krantz—the packer.

JULIE. Oh! Julius Krantz.

GIL. Very fine woman, and most entertaining.

JULIE. I'm sure.

GIL. They're stopping at the Ritz. I thought we'd dine together Sunday night—the four of us—they're getting tickets for a concert some place—she used to be quite a harpist, you know.

JULIE. No, I didn't.

GIL. Of course it'll be wonderful for you—having her only thirty miles from us. She'll be company for you while I'm off at the mines.

JULIE. Mines?

GIL. Though for that matter, you'd be perfectly safe alone. There are fifteen house servants and most of them have been there for years. Old Sebastian, for example. Do you know what he'll do, if necessary? He'll sleep on the floor outside your door all night.

JULIE. Oh, no—really, I'd rather he didn't. You see, I'd start getting sorry for him, and I'd give him one of my pillows, and then a blanket, and pretty soon I'd be out there and he'd be in the bed.

GIL. *(A mirthless laugh)* But the place you'll love—is England, Julie. The absolute quiet of it—you know English people—they never intrude. I don't see any of the county people except Hubert Randolph. He and Lady Randolph have the Wyckhamshire place. Isn't a finer man in England, to my way of thinking. And very amusing. Anybody who says the English haven't got a sense of humor doesn't know Randolph. He'll stand there, sober as a judge—you won't think he's going to say a word—suddenly he'll get off something that'll make you laugh every time you think of it.

JULIE. Such as what?

(DOOR Bell.)

GIL. Oh, I don't know. It isn't what he says, so much as the way he says it. He's a great fellow. One thing I've found, Julie, is that for real people you've got to go to—— *(Door bell rings.)*

JULIE. *(Relieved at the interruption)* Oh, that's the baby, I guess. Gwen! I guess this is the baby!

(GIL *and* JULIA *go right.)*

GIL. Huh! Oh! Gwen's baby. (JO *enters door left. Goes to outer door.)*

JULIE. Where do you want him, you people? Here's the baby!

(WOLFE *and* GWEN *enter, the former with his arm about* GWEN'S *shoulder. She is smiling up at him, he looking down at her. They have evidently been having a chummy conversation.)*

WOLFE. *(On the entrance)* . . . and I know what I'm talking about.

JULIE. Say, what are you two so chummy about?

WOLFE. We two? We got our secrets. *(To* GWEN) Ain't we?

GWEN. Big guilty ones.

WOLFE. You bet we have! You go ahead—relax. We get along.

(JO *has opened the outer door. There is heard a bedlam of barking—more than one dog, certainly. Sounds of voices—"Quiet there! Down! Shut up! What's the matter with you."*

JO. *(A voice off)* Well, who'd of thought . . . What! . . .

JULIE. Good heavens! What's that! What is it!

(There appears in the hallway two HALLBOYS *laden with baggage—bags—boxes—a sun machine and a monkey in a cage—next the tall, sinister figure of* GUNGA. *He is an East Indian, wearing his native costume, with turban. On his shoulder is a brilliant-hued bird as large as a parrot. He stands silent after his entrance. This figure is greeted with a little involuntary shriek of terror from* JULIE.)

JULIE. Oh! What's that!
GWEN. Oh, look at him!
WOLFE. Say, what in God's name! . . .
GIL. What's going on?

(TONY *enters. Ahead of him, straining at the leash, are two huge police dogs.* TONY *wears a dashing top coat of camel's hair, and a light felt hat with a brush or feather in it, of the sort one sees in the Austrian Tyrol. On his entrance he is admonishing the dogs.)*

TONY. Here, here! Where're you going? Not so fast!
JULIE. Tony! Tony!
WOLFE. Tony! Is it you!
GWEN. Why, Tony!

(FANNY *enters.* DEAN, KITTY *and* PERRY *follow in the background. Following close on* TONY *is* JO. *The luggage is of surprising size, quantity and richness.)*

TONY. *(Casually)* Hello, Sis! How've you been? . . . Hi, Gwen . . . Oscar . . . Say, Jo, got any beefsteak? *(Indicates dogs.)*
JULIE. Tony, where have you come from? Why didn't you let us know?

(JO *takes the dogs from* TONY *and goes off right with them.* DELLA *comes running on, right. There now follows a babel of greetings, exclamations.)*

FANNY. Tony! For God's sake!
KITTY. How did you get here?
DEAN. Of all the surprises!
GWEN. Why didn't you radio?

TONY. Hush, my pretties! Tell you all about it in a minute. All the fascinating facts. *(He turns to the Indian servant)* Gunga!

GUNGA. Waguha!

TONY. Mem singha salah ronhamar. Pondero mulah giva. Salah Singha Ronhamar. Gahlef! Della, show him where to go, will you?

DELLA. *(Awed)* Yes, sir.

(JO *re-enters at right. Helps with the luggage. During the next few speeches,* DELLA, GUNGA *and the* HALLBOY *and* JO *carry everything upstairs. Exit center of balcony.* TONY *gives his coat and hat to* JO *as he passes.)*

FANNY. Is he going to stay in the house?

TONY Gunga? He saved my life over in India. Another minute and the tiger'd have had me.

JULIE. Tony, what do you mean by doing a thing like this! Bursting in on us this way! Why didn't you let us know!

TONY. I was afraid to let you know. That's why I came by way of Canada. I landed in Canada.

FANNY, DEAN, GWEN, KITTY. Canada!

JULIE. Why?

TONY. Because Albania and Schlesingen were going to declare war on each other. I knew if I got out she'd marry him and everything would be all right.

JULIE. Who'd marry whom!

FANNY. What's that!

DEAN. What's he talking about?

GWEN. He's making it up.

TONY. It's been in the papers! Natalia broke off her engagement with Rupert of Schlesingen. Then the Albanians . . .

JULIE. Wait a minute!

GWEN. Hold on!

KITTY. Who is she?

DEAN. Natalia!

WOLFE. Natalia! Natalia!

FANNY. Who's Natalia?

TONY. Natalia's the Princess of Albania. She's a nice kid, but God! I didn't mean anything serious. That's the trouble with those princesses. Sheltered lives. Dance with 'em a couple of times and they want to elope with you. Of course, when she broke off with Rupert, and the Prime Minister sent for me——

JULIA. Oh! I'm beginnirg to understand. You've started an European war.

(PERRY *during this speech joins* GIL, *right.)*

TONY. Oh, I don't think they'll fight. She'll get over it. . . . Anyhow, that isn't why I came home. Oscar, listen! I was cruising around the Bayer-strasse in Koenigsberg one night, and I happened to pass a little theatre. Stuck away in a courtyard. There was a poster of this thing outside. I started to read it—I don't know, I got a hunch about it, and went in. (GIL *and* PERRY *find their interest in this narrative flagging. They stand a little apart from the group, hands in pockets, thoughtful.)* Well, say!

WOLFE. Good, huh?

TONY. Good? It's the God-damnedest play I ever saw in my life, and I bought it. You're to wire 'em three thousand dollars to-morrow. American money.

WOLFE. You bought it?

FANNY. What for?

JULIE. Yes, what for?

TONY. What for? I'm going to act in it, of course.

GWEN. Really?

FANNY. Well, that's fine. *(Rises, goes to* TONY.)

DEAN. I'm glad of that, Tonv.

WOLFE. You don't say. *(He turns to see the effect of this revelation on* JULIE. *She is mildly stunned.)*

JULIE. Tony, you don't mean pictures? You're going back on the stage?

KITTY. Of course. *(To* TONY*)* Don't you?

TONY. Do I? Wait till you see this play, Oscar. Reinhardt's going to do it in Berlin, and Pitoeff's got the French rights.

WOLFE. Well, what's it all about? What's so wonderful?

TONY. Look! I'll show you. *(As this account gets under way* GIL *and* PERRY *withdraw a little further from the group. Presently their eyes meet; these is a flash of understanding between them. In a moment they are deep in conversation. For the present, however, they are drowned by* TONY'S *voice)* If this doesn't bowl you over, I'll go back to the Ganges. *(He is pulling a pile of assorted papers out of his pocket. He turns* FANNY'S *chair back to audience, placing his papers on it. Quickly selects the one he wants; lets the others drop to the ground.)* Where the devil—oh, yes. *(Spreads one of them out. They all crowd around.)* Now here's the scene plan. Of course you can't make anything out of this, but I'll show you how it works.

KITTY. What's that there?

TONY. In the first place, they use this new constructivist scenery—grouping the actors on different levels and playing one scene up there and another one down here.

DEAN. Oh, my God!

GWEN. That new German stuff!

TONY. You don't enter or exit in the ordinary sense—you just slide, or else let down by wires. Schwenger, the fellow that does it in Koenigsberg, fainted six times the first night. When they want to show a different scene all they do is switch off the lights down here, switch them on up here. In goes this level, out goes that! It's got every trick of the motion pictures, plus another dimension. Now here's the big kick. See that? Where my finger is?

DEAN. Yes?

KITTY. Yes!

(As they all crane their necks there is just an instant's complete silence. The voice of GIL, *talking to* PERRY, *comes up.)*

GIL. And that way we cut our overhead fourteen per cent.

TONY. *(As he picks up again, the voice of* GIL *is once more drowned.* GIL, *in another second, ends his talk with* PERRY, *waits with some impatience for a chance to have a word with* JULIE.*)* That swings the whole thing around—the audience becomes the actors and the actors become the audience.

JULIE. Serves 'em right.

TONY. I tell you it's a knock-out. Of course the great thing about this play is it takes two nights to do it.

FANNY. Two nights!

DEAN. Tony, my boy!

KITTY. I never heard of such a thing.

WOLFE. Only two?

GWEN. You're cuckoo, Tony.

TONY. Now wait a minute. You don't understand what this thing is. It's a modern version of the Passion Play.

WOLFE. *(Fearfully)* And you play—what?

TONY. The lead, of course. It's pure blank verse, and the incidental music—listen. *(He dashes up to the piano, followed by the eager group. Seats himself.)* There's a sacrificial motif runs right through —tear your heart out—— *(He strikes a single chord. Is about to proceed when* GIL *breaks in.)*

GIL. Ah—Tony—Julie, before you start——

JULIE. Huh? . . . Wait a minute, Tony. . . . Yes, Gil?

(TONY *stops playing. They all pay polite but impatient attention.)*

GIL. If you people don't mind—I'm awfully sorry—I've got to break away, Julie. . . . Glad you're back, Tony, but I've got about an hour's business.

JULIE. Oh, must you go, Gil? I——

GIL. Well, I'll be right back. Later, I thought, perhaps we could. . . .

PERRY. Gwen, I think I'll have to go, too . . . seeing this fellow . . . you'll be home, huh?

GWEN. Of course, Perry.

PERRY. Well, then, I'll——

GIL. Good-bye, everybody. Good-bye. *(A chorus of heedless good-byes from the group.)* Good-bye. . . . Oh, Julie. Where would you like to dine?

JULIE. Huh!

GIL. Where would you like to dine?

JULIE. Oh, Gil, I don't think I'll go out to dinner to-night. I think I'd better—Tony here—if you don't mind——

GIL. I understand. That's all right. I'll call for you at the theatre at eleven. (GIL *and* PERRY *exit outer door.)*

JULIE. *(As he goes)* Uh—yes. . . . *(She stands apart from the rest, thoughtful, silent.)*

TONY. *(Picking it up on high)* Now, here's the way this thing goes. *(He plays a few impressive chords)* Then when he comes down from the mountain there's a stunning passage—— *(He goes into something subdued and wistful.)*

(He plays for a moment. FANNY, DEAN, KITTY *and* GWEN *are leaning over the piano.* WOLFE

stands a little apart from the others, down center, but his head is turned toward TONY, *and his attention is on him.* JULIE *comes down right of* WOLFE, *puts a hand on his arm to attract his attention.* WOLFE *turns to* JULIE, *slowly.)*

JULIE. Oscar——

WOLFE. *(Rather absently)* Huh?

JULIE. Why don't you let me read the play?

WOLFE. What?

JULIE. That play by your college professor—— Why don't you let me read it?

WOLFE. What do you mean, read it? What for?

JULIE. Why, I just thought I'd like to, that's all. To sort of get an idea of the part.

WOLFE. I'll send you up a manuscript this evening. *(The music ceases; there is a chorus of exclamation and admiration from the group.)*

GWEN. Oh, that's thrilling!

FANNY. Gives me goose-flesh.

DEAN. Very nice—very nice, indeed!

KITTY. Goes right throught you!

TONY. But the biggest kick of all comes in the fire-worship scene in the eighth act. They've got a religious procession there, lasts twelve minutes, and, believe me, it's pretty pagan! Oscar, if you can get by with that and not be padlocked—— *(Strikes a chord or two. Sings "Boom! Boom!"* DELLA *enters, goes to door.)*

(DOOR Bell.)

(MISS PEAKE, *the nurse, enters from outer door with the baby in her arms.* DELLA *follows and crosses left.)*

JULIE. It's the baby! Look! It's the baby!

(The group breaks. They leave TONY *and the piano*

and surround the baby. There is a good deal of clucking and kitzakitzing and those strange noises with which adults seek to divert the helpless infant. Overlap these speeches.)

KITTY. Isn't he darling?

JULIE. Tony, look! You've never seen him before!

BERT. Well, what do you think of him?

FANNY. Give him to me. Give him to me. *(He is passed over to her)* Well! There you are! *(Comes center.)*

KITTY. He *is* cute!

TONY. *(Rises from piano)* I think he's terrible. *(Sits as before.)*

FANNY. *(Standing the baby in one arm. Indicates the portrait of* AUBREY CAVENDISH *on the wall)* Do you know who that is, young man? You were named for him. Aubrey Cavendish Stewart, and see that you live up to it. . . .

JULIE. Mother, do you think you ought to hold him?

FANNY. Now, now! I guess I can hold a baby!

WOLFE. Here you are. Sit down. (FANNY *sits in her chair, her back to audience.)*

KITTY. Ooooooo! Who you staring at, ooo big eyes! Ooo great big eyes sing!

GWEN. Miss Peake, don't you want to take his coat off?

MISS PEAKE. I think it's a bit chilly in here, Mrs. Stewart.

KITTY. Oh, he can't keep his coat on.

JULIE. Let's take him in by the fire.

DELLA. *(At tea table)* Another cocktail, Mr. Dean. (DEAN *crosses and takes cocktail.)*

GWEN. We've got to take him in by the fire, people.

WOLFE. *(Stooping to survey the baby)* Say, that

young fellow is a Cavendish, all right! He can't deny that!

DEAN. By Jove, Fanny! He does look like Aubrey!

KITTY. Do you think he'll be an actor?

WOLFE. Say, he shouldn't be an actor! Look at him! *(A sudden idea. A snap of the fingers.)* Here's an idea!

GWEN. Yes? What?

WOLFE. Listen, show folks! I got a great new play I'm going to produce—*(A side look at* JULIE*)*—and in it they talk all the time about a baby. Why shouldn't we have a scene where the baby is carried on, and—— *(A gesture toward the baby.* DELLA *comes center with tray of cocktails.)*

GWEN. You're crazy, Wolfey! Perry wouldn't hear of it.

JULIE. Gwen, he'll have to start *some* time.

FANNY. Certainly will!

DEAN. *(Holding up his cocktail glass and signalling the others to join him)* Here's to Aubrey Cavendish Stewart! *(A chorus of assent from the others. A little rush for the cocktails.)*

ALL. Yes! Yes! Aubrey!

TONY. *(Gives a glass to* FANNY*)* Here you are, Fanny! *(Holds aloft his glass)* To the kid!

FANNY. *(The child in her arm. Takes the glass in her hand. Holds it aloft)* To Aubrey Cavendish!

GWEN. Stewart!

FANNY. That won't stop him! He's a Cavendish, and he's going to carry on! We always have, and we always will. "When one drops out there's always another one to take his place. When one drops out there's always been another" . . .

JULIE. Now, mother . . .

FANNY. To the future greatest actor of his day! Aubrey Cavendish Second! *(They all drink.)*

MISS PEAKE. I really think, Mrs. Stewart——

GWEN. *(Takes the child from* FANNY*)* Yes. All right, Miss Peake. Come on, everybody. He's got to go in where it's warm.

(A general movement toward the library door. More clucking and hubbub over the child. "Look! He's laughing! . . . Here we go! . . .He knows what it's all about. . . .")

TONY. Wait till you hear the ballet music, you people! How's this piano?

JULIE. Come on, mother dear.

(All except FANNY *exit into library. The noise goes on from there, fainter, of course, but still heard, very merry.* TONY *is playing some gay strains on the off-stage piano.* FANNY *has remained in her chair. As the others have passed into the next room, she now attempts to rise, her cane falls from her hand and she sinks back in the chair.)*

DELLA. *(When the cane falls.* DELLA *counts eight and enters)* Isn't he the cute one, though? *(She exits into library.)*

(After DELLA *exits,* FANNY *slowly lifts the glass to the picture of her late husband,* AUBREY CAVENDISH. *She again attempts to rise, but the glass falls to the floor and the hand that held it drops to the side—and her head falls forward. There is a moment's pause. The voices from the next room come up, high and gay, and there is laughter, and chirping to the baby.)*

GWEN. *(Voice from the library)* Where's Fanny?

JULIE. Where's Mother? . . . Mother, come on in. See what he's doing now! Mother, where are you? *(Appears in library doorway.)* Mother, come on in. He just did the cutest—— *(Stops, startled, at something queer in the figure huddled in the chair. Comes quickly, fearfully, crosses to the chair, one hand outstretched. Comes around in front of chair. Touches* FANNY. *Calls)* Gwen! Tony! Oscar!

(At the note in her voice they come, streaming in slowly, talking a little, perhaps, in a subdued tone, and rather apprehensive. At look in JULIE'S *face they are warned. Their faces take on a stricken look. Awed, fearful, they tiptoe toward the still form in the chair.)*

CURTAIN.

FURNITURE AND DECORATIONS

ACT I

The following pieces of furniture are numbered to correspond with the numbers on the scene design.

No. 1. Mahogany inlaid gate-leg table, on which are:

2 Magazines.
1 Gold frame with Julie's photo.
1 Glass cigarette holder with cigarettes.
1 Match box with matches.
1 Metal vase with white narcissus.
1 Glass ash tray.

No. 2. Upholstered bench with:

1 Opened magazine.

No. 3. Chintz-covered armchair with:

1 Tan satin pillow.

No. 4. Small coffee table (tray top) with:

2 Magazines.

No. 5. Maple commode (low boy) with:

1 Card tray (silver).
1 Glass table lamp, with glass shade.

No. 6. Straight back side chair (Louis XIV).

No. 7. Large walnut secretary with:

1 Desk blotter in leather case.
1 Desk set and writing paper, envelopes, etc.
1 Large glass vase with white Chrysanthemums.
6 Unmounted photos of Julie.
1 Table lamp, parchment shade.

No. 8. Side chair (rush seat).

No. 9. Piano bench (upholstered).
No. 10. Grand piano, on which are:
1 Green damask cope.
20 Sheets of music.
1 Copy New York "Times."
1 Glass ash tray.
1 Glass cigarette container.
1 Leather photo grame with Julie's photo.
1 French telephone with extra long receiver cord.
4 Magazines.
1 Large yellow urn with light yellow and orange.
1 Table lamp. Gold embossed base. Parchment shade.
No. 11. Chintz covered sofa (same design as chair No. 3) with:
2 Chintz pillows (same design as sofa).
2 Tan pillows (satin).
1 Glass ash tray is on back of the sofa.
No. 12. Lightweight sewing table with drawer. With:
1 Deck cards in drawer.
No. 13. Victorian chair. Upholstered in black with cutout design. With:
1 Brocade sewing bag hangs on the back of this chair. Sewing material in bag.
No. 14. Armchair (tapestry covered Louis XV).
No. 15. Mahogany (round top) tip table. With:
1 Square metal vase with tan and purple asters.
3 Magazines.
1 Empty match box in green case.
1 Cigarette container—cigarettes.
1 Glass ash tray.
No. 16. Small bench (10x16), Old English. With:
2 Magazines.

No. 17. Waste basket (old drum).

No. 18. Large red lacquer commode with marble top. With:

1 Large vase with pink roses.
4 Magazines.
1 Gold frame with Julie's photo.
1 Match box with matches.
In top drawer 25 cigarettes.
1 Table lamp. Yellow urn base. Parchment shade.

No. 19. Straight back Louis XV chair.

No. 20. Coffee table. With:

1 Combination ash tray and match holder.
1 Box matches.

No. 21. High Venetian table (12x12) with:

1 Yellow urn with green leaves.

No. 22. Hepplewhite side chair. Upholstered in striped rose silk.

No. 23. Large wing chair.

No. 24. Upright piano.

No. 25. Piano stool.

No. 26. (On balcony) Hepplewhite chair same as No. 22.

No 27. (On balcony) Venetian console table, marble top. With:

1 Glass vase with old rose asters.

No. 28. (On balcony) Antique cabinet. With:

1 Metal candelabra.

Outside of Window Right:

3 Sections of hedge.
1 Hedge tree.

Wall Decorations

Over commode No. 5 is a large mirror (metal).
Over chair No. 8 is a small landscape.
Over commode No. 18 is a very large oil of Aubrey Cavendish.

Over chair No. 26 is picture of flowers.
Over table No. 27 is a French mirror, size 14x16.

Portiers

At window Right: Ecru net, over which is dark green, tan satin lined curtains, with valence. Wood carved tie-backs embossed in gold hold these curtains in place.

Off stage Left: Ecru net over which is rose striped silk lined with blue satin. These are held back by two gold rosettes. There is a wood valance over these curtains.

ACT II

For this Act there is a slight change in the furniture and flowers.

Chair No. 14 is struck (removed from the set).

Table No. 15 is moved up stage.

Bench No. 16 is brought down in place of table No. 15. Remove magazines.

Waste basket No. 17 is brought down to lower side of commode No. 18.

Table No. 20 is placed below library door.

Table No. 21 is placed up stage next to waste basket. On this table is placed:

200 addressed, stamped and sealed letters of different color, tints and sizes. Also a small vase to break. The flowers that were on table No. 1 are struck and the vase of green leaves now stand on this table.

The vase of white chrysanthemums that were on the secretary are now replaced by a vase of red poppies.

The vase with the purple asters that stood on table No. 15 are now on table No. 20 below the library door.

The asters that were on the balcony are replaced by yellow chrysanthemums. The other flowers remain the same.

Three magazines, a tennis racket and a fencing mask are lying on the floor down right, near table No. 1.

A golf stick is on the floor in front of sofa.

ACT III

The furniture in this set is back to the same positions as in Act I, except table No. 21 is near the X left balustrade of the stairs. There is a lace cover on the table.

Chair No. 14 is brought on and put in its former place.

Table No. 15 is brought down and a fountain pen, 6 merchant's bills with checks made out for Julie to sign, also 6 addressed envelopes.

Chair No. 3 is shoved against the left wall.

Chair No. 6 is placed in the hallway next to commode No. 5.

The top of the piano is open for this Act.

Strike Julie's picture from table No. 1.

Strike sewing bag on chair No. 13.

Tabie No. 20 is again above the door.

As this Act is one year later, remove all the flowers.

Take the green leaves from table No. 1 and place them on the balcony, replacing the chrysanthemums.

Two dozen American Beauty roses in a tall glass vase stand on the piano.

Easter lilies and dark red roses are on the secretary No. 7 and on the commode No. 18.

Calla lilies and green leaves are on table No. 1.

SIDE PROPS AND HAND PROPS

ACT I

Props off hallway Entrance Right:
- 1 Silver card tray on commode.
- 1 Telegram in envelope.
- 1 Manuscript of a play (The Conqueror).
- 1 Violin case.
- 1 Leather net box.
- 1 Steamer rug.
- 1 Golf bag and clubs.
- 4 Dress suit cases.
- 2 Tennis rackets with covers.

Props under the balcony (Servants' Entrance):
- Tray No. 1 with tray cloth:
  - Dishes.
  - Napkin covering same.
- Tray No. 11 with tray cloth:
  - Cup and saucer.
  - Knife, fork and spoon.
  - Sugar bowl with sugar.
  - Cream pitcher with cream.
  - Plate of toast.
  - Coffee pot with coffee.
  - Napkin.
- Tray No. 3 with tray cloth.
  - Cup and saucer.
  - Knife, fork and spoon.
  - Sugar bowl with sugar.
  - Cream pitcher with cream.
  - Coffee pot with coffee.
  - Plate of toast.

Plate with scrambled eggs and bacon.
Butter.
Napkin.

Tray No. 4 with tray cloth:
Cup and saucer.
Knife, fork and spoon.
Sugar bowl with sugar.
Cream pitcher with cream.
Coffee pot with coffee.
Plate of toast.
Two plates of eggs and bacon.
Butter.
Napkin.

NOTE: After this tray has been placed on stage, one plate of eggs is transferred to tray No. 2 (Dean's tray).

Tray No. 5:
Small round tray with doily.
Silver goblet with milk.

Tray No. 6:
Small tray with doily.
Plate of rolls.

Tray No. 7:
Tray with tray cloth.
2 Dishes with silver covers, one of these dishes contains bacon and eggs.
Knife, fork and spoon.
One folded napkin.
One napkin to cover over dishes.

NOTE: The trays are different sizes and shapes. The dishes are of silver and good chinaware.

Ladies' hat box with C.O.D. tag attached.
Large flower box (American Beauty rose size) tied with red ribbon.
Three stacks of boxes (about 6 boxes in each pile).
These boxes are from the best shops and

are of different sizes, shapes and colors. Dress, hat, shirtwaist, flower boxes, etc.

Props on balcony off right center (Julie's room):
- Telegram.
- Pair boxing gloves.
- Pair shoes.
- 6 Prop dresses.
- Black leather bag.

Props on balcony off left center (Fanny's room):
- Tray with tray cloth.
- Dirty dishes.
- Coffee pot.
- Plate with two pieces toast.
- Soiled napkin.
- Snowshoe.

Props off left (library):
- Pair boxing gloves.

Personal props:
- Cigarette case and cigarettes, pocket lighter for Dean.
- Cigarette case and cigarettes, pocket lighter for Kitty.
- Bill fold and money for Oscacr.
- Money (bills) for Jo.
- Money (bills) for Bellboy.
- Money (bills) for Chauffeur.

ACT II

Under balcony (servants' entrance):
- Silver flask.
- Drinking glass.
- Tray with tray cloth and cup of hot broth.
- 10 pieces of wood for fireplace.

On balcony off right center (Julie's room):
- Hot water bag.
- Medicine kit.

On balcony off left center (Fanny's room):
- Damask towel.

On balcony off extreme left (Tony's room):
  Quart bottle.
  Violin case, leather hat box, steamer rug, 3 dress suit cases, golf bag and clubs, tennis racket, same as Act One.
Props off left (library):
  Manuscript of play (Mrs. Castlemane).
Side props:
  Tennis racket.
  Fencing mask.
  Golf club.
Personal props:
  Money (bills—perhaps $2,000 held together by paper band, for Oscar).
  Fencing foil, mask and glove for McDermott.
  Fencing foil and glove for Tony.
  Cane for Fanny.

ACT III

Hand props off door right (hallway):
  2 Dress suit cases with European hotel stickers.
  1 Sun machine.
  1 Violin case, same as previous acts.
  1 Leather hat box.
  1 Large green parrot.
  1 Monkey in cage.
  2 German police dogs.
  1 Infant doll, dressed.
Hand props off center (Servants' Entrance):
  Tray with tray cloth and
    Silver teapot with spirit lamp.
    Cake plate with 6 slices of cake.
  Large silver tray with lace tray cloth and
    Silver tea service.
  Tray with tray cloth and

Silver cocktail shaker with ginger ale and ice.
9 cocktail glasses.
Cake dish with gingerbread or dark cake.
12 Lunch plates for Jo.

Side props on tip up table No. 15:
1 Fountain pen.
6 Tradesman's bills with checks attached.
6 Envelopes.

Personal props:
Hand bag for Fanny.
Blueprint for Tony.
Timetables for Tony.
Cane for Fanny, same as before.

PROP LIST

1 Large walnut secretary.
1 Red lacquered commode.
2 Hepplewhite chairs.
1 Upholstered bench.
2 Antique side chairs (Louis XV).
1 English bench (stool).
1 Mahogany tip top table.
1 Inlaid (walnut) gateleg table.
1 Piano bench (upholstered).
1 Grand piano.
1 Tapestry armchair (Louis XVI).
1 Side chair (rush seat).
1 Small coffee table (tray top).
1 Oval sewing table.
1 Victorian chair.
1 Chintz overstuffed sofa.
1 Chintz overstuffed chair to match.
1 Venetian console table (marble top).
1 Small maple commode (lowboy).
1 Large winged armchair.
1 Coffee table.
1 High Venetian table.
1 Antique cabinet.
1 Upright piano and stool.
2 Gold wood carved photo frames.
1 Green damask cope.
3 Yellow urns.
1 Large urn.
3 Glass cigarette holders.
4 glass ash trays.
3 green metal match box holders.

14 Magazines.
12 Sheets music.
1 New York "Times."
1 French telephone.
1 Leather photo frame.
3 photos of Julie for frames.
6 photos of Julie.
1 Wall mirror.
1 French wall mirror.
1 Small landscape.
1 Large painting (flowers).
1 Life size oil in heavy frame (Aubrey Cavendish).
6 Prop dresses.
1 Hot water bag.
1 Medicine case.
1 Ground cloth.
1 Stair carpet.
2 pieces carpet 6x8.
1 Piece carpet for balcony (carpets are all terra cotta).
1 Metal candelabra.
1 Leather desk set.
1 Whiskey flask.
1 Drinking glass.
1 Pair ladies' shoes.
1 Damask towel.
1 Snowshoe.
6 dress suit cases (2 with foreign stickers).
1 Leather bag.
1 Leather hat box.
1 Violin case.
1 Steamer rug.
20 Fancy boxes.
1 Flower box tied with red ribbon.
1 Ladies' hat box with C.O.D. tab.
1 Silver goblet.
1 Silver cocktail shaker.
10 Serving trays (different sizes).

1 Silver tray.
12 Lunch plates.
4 Dinner plates.
3 China covered dishes.
3 China cups and saucers.
1 China soup cup and plate.
3 Small plates.
3 Silver sugar bowls.
3 Silver cream pitchers.
1 Silver coffee pot.
2 nickel plate covers.
9 Cocktail glasses (extra ones to break).
4 China coffee pots.
150 Sheets stage money.
200 Letters addressed and stamped.
1 Fountain pen.
6 Checks.
12 napkins.
10 tray cloths.
5 fancy pillows.
1 quart bottle.
1 sun machine.
10 vases of different sizes.
1 Billfold.
2 Cigarette cases.
2 Pocket lighters.
1 Blue print (Tony).
6 Timetables (Tony).
2 Sets boxing gloves (4).
1 Plasstron.
2 Fencing gloves.
2 fencing foils.
2 Masks.
3 Tennis rackets (2 with covers).
1 Golf bag.
6 Golf clubs.
4 Table knives, forks, teaspoons.
10 pieces of wood for fireplace.

1 Pair green portiers and valance.
1 Pair pink striped silk portiers.
2 Pair net curtains.
2 Gold tie backs.
1 Pair gold rosettes.
1 Parrot cage.
Silver card tray.
Telegraph envelopes.
Telegraph blanks.
Brocade sewing bag with sewing.
Vase to break for each performance.
Match holder and tray.
Cane for Fanny.
Fountain pen.
Check book.
6 Tradesmen's billheads.
Writing paper and envelopes.
2 Manuscripts of plays.
Infant doll, dressed.
Waste basket.

Live Stock

1 monkey.
1 parrot.
2 police dogs.

Perishable Props

4 orders scrambled eggs.
4 orders bacon.
4 orders toast.
3 Cups of coffee.
1 Pint milk.
4 Small rolls.
6 Slices ginger bread.
6 pieces cake.
1 Quart ginger ale.

Small piece ice.
Sugar.
1 Cup of tea for broth.

Flowers

2 Dozen American Beauty roses.
2 Dozen dark velvet roses.
1 Dozen yellow chrysanthemums.
1 Dozen white chrysanthemums.
4 Dozen Easter lilies.
1 Dozen calla lilies.
2 Dozen dark yellow asters (large).
1 Dozen dark purple asters (small).
3 Dozen orange lady slippers (velvet).
3 Dozen light yellow lady slippers (muslin)
2 Dozen pink roses.
2 Dozen yellow poppies.
2 Dozen white narcissus.
2 Large bunches green leaves.

TELEPHONE, DOORBELL AND BUZZER CUES

ACT I

Curtain Up—

Della enters on balcony, as she descends stairs (ring telephone) until she answers.

Della—"Hello" (Buzzer twice).

Della—"Yes, I'll take—dinner at Mrs. Sherwins" (Buzzer once).

Della—"Just what we need" (Phone).

McDermott—"G'wan" (Doorbell).

Della—As she places boxes on bench and starts for door (Phone rings and continues ringing until Della answers).

Della—"I'll tell her" (Buzzer once).

Della—"Give me those" (Buzzer once).

Jo—"Upwards of ten ye" (Doorbell twice).

Dean—"Getting long in years" (Doorbell).

Kitty—"I'd be marvelous in that part" (Della enters and as she descends stairs) (Ring phone until she answers).

Dean—"Julia and Gwen in their play" (Doorbell twice).

Julia—As she leads Kitty and Dean in library—closes door—then leans against door frame (Phone rings twice).

Fanny—"Let it ring" (Phone continues until Julie answers).

Gwen—"Then I'll be acting" (Doorbell twice).

Gwen—"I'll be an old woman" (Doorbell twice).

Chauffeur—As he is coming down stairs (Doorbell twice).
Tony—"Ah! Lunch!" (Phone).

ACT II

Fanny—"Look out for Poles" (Phone once). As Tony places receiver back on hook (Ring again).
Julie—"I've got my art to attend to" (Doorbell twice).
Dean—"Just a few weeks" (Doorbell sharply 3 times).
Julie—"Spirits of ammonia, bring the whole thing" (As Della comes down stairs, doorbell twice).
Julie—"We're going to be together" (Phone once).
Gil—"Thea ought to be exciting" (Phone till Julie answers).
Gil—"Good-bye" (Buzzer).

ACT III

Fanny—"And Kitty" (Doorbell).
Fanny—"Kitty" (Doorbell).
Gwen—"It will be dandy" (Doorbell).
Gil—"You've got to go to——" (Doorbell).
Tony—"Lasts twelve minutes" (Doorbell twice).

COSTUMES

FANNY

Act I:

White wig—elaborate morning cream teagown with cream taffeta coat trimmed in lace with de Medici collar. Cream slippers.

Act II:

First Entrance:

Black satin gown—black shoes. White Spanish shawl. Cane.

Second Entrance:

Cream wrapper or nightgown—lace cap with light gray kimono—cream slippers.

Act III:

Purple house gown—purple slippers.

JULIE

Act I:

Black velvet dress—black velvet hat—beige suede gloves, bag, black shoes, and black pointed fox neck fur. Tan stockings.

Act II:

Beige velvet gown—henna velvet coat, trimmed in red fox, henna felt hat—tan handbag—tan kid gloves—gold mules—tan satin shoes—tan stockings.

Act III:

Pink chiffon tea gown, shoes and stockings.

GWEN

Act I:
First Entrance:
Riding suit—tan Todphore trousers—tan Todphore boots. Buff vest. Brown coat. White shirtwaist with attached collar. Four-in-hand tie. Brown felt hat.
Second Entrance:
Same trousers—gold mules—figured silver cloth dressing coat trimmed in orange velvet.
Third Entrance:
Canary colored crepe dress—black velvet hat and coat.
Act II:
Pink negligee petal trimmed with edges picoted in silver. Pink mules and stockings.
Act III:
Pea green woolen crepe dress piped in white braid. Pea green felt hat. Tan shoes and stockings. Squirrel fur coat. Green and gray handbag. White gloves.

KITTY

Act I:
Wine red velvet dress—hat and shoes to match—tan handbag and stockings. Brown fox neckpiece—carries gloves.
Act II:
Black satin skirt. Sage green blouse—green felt hat. Mink fur coat. Black shoes—tan stockings—white gloves.
Act III:
Black velvet dress, pearl trimming. Black hat, shoes, handbag. Stockings. White gloves.

DELLA

Act I:

Maid's uniform. Gray dress. White cap. Collars, cuffs and apron.

Act II:

The same.

Act III:

Black uniform.

MISS PEAK

Nursemaid's uniform. Black outfit with veil head-dress—white collars, cuffs, etc.

TONY

Act I:

First Entrance:

Gray lounge suit, gray fur coat, gray hat, tan shoes, black silk muffler for sling.

Second Entrance:

Turkish bathrobe, gray trousers, tan shoes.

Act II:

First Entrance:

White trousers with pin stripe, white shirt with attached collar, rubber sole shoes, fencing glove.

Second Entrance:

Same trousers, same shirt, black shoes.

Third Entrance:

Same.

Fourth Entrance:

Silk robe, B.V.D.'s (underwear), black shoes.

Fifth Entrance:

Bellboy's uniform, black shoes.

ACT III:

Gray lounge suit—gray overcoat—Alpine hat with feather.

OSCAR

ACT I:

Dark gray lounge suit, gray top coat, black velour hat, cane, black shoes.

ACT II:

Same suit as Act One. Black top coat which is not removed. Velour hat—black shoes.

ACT III:

Dark Oxford coat and vest, black striped trousers, black shoes. Black velour hat, carries an overcoat.

DEAN

ACT I:

Gray lounge suit, black top coat, black derby hat, black shoes, cane.

ACT II:

Same as Act I.

ACT III:

Gray morning coat and vest. Striped trousers. Black shoes, gray top coat. Cane. He wears a toupee in this act.

MARSHALL

ACT II:

Dinner suit, black top coat, black hat.

ACT III:

Gray striped lounge suit.

PERRY

ACT I:

Smart riding suit with boots and gray top coat. Soft hat—gloves.

Second Entrance:
Black lounge suit—carrying top coat and hat.
ACT II:
Black lounge suit, top coat, hat.
ACT III:
Brown lounge suit.

JO

ACT I:
White coat, military cut. Gray striped trousers. Black shoes.
ACT II:
Black alpaca coat. Black vest. Same trousers and shoes.
ACT III:
Black dress coat. Black vest and trousers. Black shoes.

McDERMOTT

ACT I:
White athletic shirt, dark blue trousers with white stripe on seam. Belt. Black shoes.
Second Entrance:
Gray lounge suit, gray top coat—black derby, black shoes.
ACT II:
Same as first dress in Act I. Fencing mask, glove and plastron.
Second Entrance:
Same as second entrance in Act I.

CHAUFFEUR

Long canvas coat, sheepskin lined—blue visor cap.

BELLBOYS

Maroon suits. Gray stripe in the trousers. Short, tight-fitting jackets with gold ball buttons. Gray band on the pill-box caps.

NOTE: The suit that TONY wears is the same as the above. The Bellboy that wears Tony's fur coat and hat in the second act slips on a pair of trouser legs that are held up by an elastic band.

GONGA

East Indian. Yellow turban. Dark red stripe smock. Yellow sash. European trousers and black shoes.

LIGHT PLOT

Key to Electric Plan

Balcony Lights:
A—Light amber, 1000 W.
B—Pink, 1000 W.
C—Light straw, 1000 W.
D—Light amber, 1000 W.
Foots:
26 Light pink, 60 W.
26 Frost, 60 W.
8 Blue, 60 W.
X Ray 2 Sections, 3 Circuits:
4—Blue—100 W. each.
4—Amber—100 W. each.
4—Frost—100 W. each.
Spots:
1 Straw frost 1000 W.
2 Light amber 1000 W.
3 Light pink 1000 W.
4 Frost 1000 W.
5 Light pink 1000 W.
6 Light pink 1000 W.
7 Light amber 1000 W.
8 Light amber 1000 W.
E—spot 1000 W. light amber.
F—spot 1000 W. blue.
G—flood 1000 W. light amber.
H—flood 100 W. blue.
I—one light strip 60 W.
J—Wall bracket—two light—15 W. with shade.
K—Table lamp 2 volt carbon.

L—Same as J.
M—Small table lamp with shade 30 W.
N—One light strip 15 W.
O—Star hall lamp (hanging) 2 volt carbon.
P—Same as N.
Q—Large table lamp with shade 60 W.
R—Large table lamp with shade 60 W.
S—Spot on extension stand—amber 1000 W.
T—Flood—1000 Act I—Amber—Act II—and three—blue.
U—Baby—red medium 250 W.
V—2 light strip 60 W. each.
W—2 ten light strip: 12 faded blue 60 each, 2 frost—in center 60 each, 6 frost—alternate 15 each.

LIGHT PLOT TO WORK SHOW

TIME: 1:30 P.M.

ACT I

Open

Foots—full up.

X Ray—3 circuits—¾ up.

Spots 1-2-3-4-5-6-7-8—¾ up.

Outside of Window Right:

1-1000 W. hanging flood—amber.

1-1000 W. spot—light amber (focussed on window).

Hallway:

1-one light strip (dead after the first act).

1 table lamp on commode (not on).

Off Left (Library):

1-2 light-strip—on for three acts.

1-250 W. baby spot (red medium). (This lamp stands on the floor and is focussed on the window and is on for three acts).

1-1000 W. flood on stand—light amber—this is back of the window.

On Balcony:

2-10 light strips ½ up (on for three acts).

Fanny's Room:

1-1 light strip frost 25 V. on 3 acts.

Julie's Room:

1-1 light strip frost 25 V. on 3 acts.

Balcony light, come up on dimmer to full.
  Dim out on as you ring first curtain.
On Stage Lamp:
  Table lamp on red commode left (not on).
  Table lamp on piano center (not on).
  Table lamp on secretary right (not on).

TIME: 6 P.M.

Act II

Opens with foots down on dimmer (just a glow).
  Amber circuit X Ray ¼ up.
  Frost circuit X Ray ¼ up.
  Blue circuit X Ray ¼ up.
  Spot No. 7—¼ up.
  Spot No. 3—¼ up.
Table lamp on commode on.
Portrait lamp on painting on.
1-1000 bunch off window R. blue medium.
1-1000 spot off window R. blue medium (focussed on window).
2 brackets in hallway on.
Table lamp in hallway on (2 volt carbon bulb).
2 balcony 10 light strips on.
Star light on—2 volt carbon bulb.
Lights in Fanny's and Julie's room on.
1-1000 W. spot on stand off left on balcony (amber) on. (This is focussed to shoot across balcony).
1-1000 W. flood, off window in library (blue).
1-2 light strip.
1 baby—fireplace light (red).
On Cue:

Foots up ½. Spot No. 5 up ½. Spot No. 2 up ½. X-ray up ½.	To cover piano lamp.

On Cue:

Foots up ¾.
Spot No. 8 ¾.
Spot No. 6 ¾.
Spot No. 4 ¾.
Spot No. 1 ¾.
X Ray—¾.
} To cover lamp on secretary.

Slow bring your balcony lights up on dimmer to full.

Act III

Same as Act II after everything has been brought up.

Note: The telephone bell, the doorbell, the house telephone and the buzzer works from a board on the prompt side of the stage.

SUGGESTED TEXT CHANGES IN "THE ROYAL FAMILY"

The following cuts and changes were made by Ellis Rabb for his highly successful Tony Award-winning revival during the '75-'77 seasons. We re-iterate that the Owners recommend most strongly that this updated version be used.

PAGE

11. 2nd line from top. CUT from Della's exit down to third line from bottom of page. Resume with stage direction (Remembers telegram. . . .)
17. 19th line from top. CUT: KITTY: . . . "I was doing—"
21. 12th line from bottom. CORRECTION: Should read: FANNY: "Invalid? I never felt better in my life . . ." etc.
22. 5th line from top. Cut the word, "Mrs."
31. 19th line from top: CORRECTION: The name is Zeta Zaydak. Correct here and all later references to her.
33. 10th line from bottom: CUT: "Everything grand."
34. 7th line from top: CUT: ". . . my girl, it is now—my God!—five minutes after two! . . ."
34. 13th line from top: CUT: ". . . I'm not so stuck on it, either, but . . ."
34. 17th line from top: CUT: "Out of a blue sky—"
34. 12th line from bottom: CUT: From "Now, now, hold on a minute—" through ". . . more of them."

34. 4th line from bottom: CUT: "We call it settled, huh? You'll be there?"
35. 11th line from top: CUT: From "The chances are . . ." through ". . . Gay Lord Quex to 'em."
36. 12th line from top: CUT: From "You got some" through Julie's line, "Oh now Oscar."
38. 4th line from bottom: CUT directions of last 4 lines of this page. Continue CUT from top of page 39 through Julie's line, "The honor of the family" (23rd line from top on p. 39).
42. 18th line from bottom: CUT: Fanny: "Shouts and murmurs off."
51. 7th line from bottom: CUT: From "Wolfe suddenly phoned" through "photographed with Mother."
53. 12th line from bottom: CUT: ". . . huh? . . . Not me!"
56. 3rd line from bottom: CUT: whole Dean & Fanny speech from "Not act again!"
57. 8th line from bottom: CUT Ad lib speeches of Dean, Fanny & Kitty.
64. 6th line from bottom: CUT: "Aubrey and Fanny Cavendish in 'A Gentleman from France'."
66. 4th line from top: CORRECTION: Should read ". . . since Little Lord Fauntleroy."
66. 17th line from top: CUT: From "I don't give a damn" to "Why didn't you say so?"

    Also CUT business that follows with waste basket.

    Resume with: Fanny: "Don't think you're fooling me. . . . etc."
67. 12th line from top: CUT: From "That's why" . . . to . . . "do you?"
67. 2nd line from bottom: CUT: "Look out for Poles!"
77. 15th line from top: CUT: "May God strike me dead if I ever appear in an all star revival!"
77. 17th line from bottom: CORRECTION: 1st sentence should read "Well, she's promised to dress and come down."
78. 19th line from bottom: CUT: "Forty-one weeks. Fifteen hundred a week."
80. 7th line from top: CUT: "Speak for yourself."
81. 19th line from bottom: CUT: From "They sent the supper" through "I ever saw him give."
83. 11th line from top: CUT Della's entrance. This will omit following lines:

    Fanny: What is it, Della?
    Della: How about dinner?
    Fanny: Don't bother us!

    Instead, scene continues with Fanny's "Yes, you've got to leave . . ."
83. 16th line from bottom: CUT: "Hobbling around with this thing." Also CUT direction re ("Brandishing her cane").
83. Bottom line. CORRECTION: Substitute "hand" for "cane."
84. 3rd line from top: CORRECTION: Substitute "Ladies and Gentlemen" for "Everybody."
84. 4th line from top: After "How's the house?", INSERT: "Ssh—."
84. 7th line from bottom: CORRECTION: Remove directions re McDermott appearing on balcony and coming downstairs.
85. 8th line from bottom: CUT: "Let me alone. I've got her." Substitute the following:

Tony: Here, mother. Let me carry you.
Fanny: No, no, I'm all right.

85. 4th line from bottom: CUT: Whole McDermott speech (from "That's the stuff").
86. 4th line from top: INSERT: After "let me carry her," Fanny says: "Of course not." (Continue as is)
86. 9th line from top: CUT: Direction ("McDermott is on her left").
86. 15th line from top: CUT direction: (Fanny faints). Substitute: (Fanny exits).
86. 16th line from top: CUT: from "Look out there" through ". . . get a doctor."
94. 8th line from bottom: After "Much obliged old Fellow," INSERT: "Come! For England!"
107. Bottom line: CUT: From "I bet he don't see . . ." through
108. ". . . cafe au lait" (on p. 108—third line from top).
109. Top line: Cut: "And purple her habiliments and scarlet was her soul."
109. 2nd line from top: After ". . . art thou, Romeo?", INSERT: "Speaking of Romeo, where's your young man?"
115. 15th line from bottom: CORRECTION: Line should read: "Marry you? It's bad enough to manage you . . ." etc.
118. Top line: After "Kitty has reached the love interest"—INSERT:
    Kitty (calling from library): Mother Cavendish—
    Fanny: *Don't* call me Mother Cavendish!
    (exits into library)
118. 3rd line from bottom: CUT: "After all . . ." through ". . . surely now."
119. 4th line from bottom. CUT: ". . . in the last twenty years."
121. 14th line from top: CORRECTION: Should read, "I can't, Oscar. I can't."
123. 18th line from top: CUT from ". . . sleep all the time" through "four minutes a day."
    Then CUT from "I'm in the way" through "but there aren't," resuming with "So here I am . . ."
127. 2nd line from top: After ". . . in my honor, too," INSERT:
    Julie: "Why, of course."
127. 6th line from bottom: After Gil's speech ending, "Manolo Berlanga." CUT: Fanny: Really?, and INSERT in its place:
    Dean and Kitty: (Simultaneously.) "Oh, Manolo Berlanga."
128. 8th line from top: CORRECTION: Should read "Seems the manager had run off with the money."
128. 3rd line from bottom: CUT from "No. You see . . ." through
129. to ". . . Come on, let's have some tea." on p. 129, 13th line from top. Resume with direction of ("Gwen exits into library," etc.).
130. 8th line from bottom: CORRECTION: After ". . . daughter of Julius Krantz—" should read: ". . . the meat packer."
131. 16th line from the top: After ". . . he'd be in the bed." INSERT:
    Gil (a puzzled laugh. Chucks her under the chin): "You devil"
131. 16th line from top: CUT: From "But the place you'll love . . ." through "He's a great fellow."
134. 14th line from top: CUT: "Is he going to stay in the house?"
134. 15th line from top: CORRECTION: Should read "Gunga saved my life . . ."
135. 17th line from bottom: CUT "There was a poster of this thing outside. I started to read—I don't know—"

137. 16th line from top: CORRECTION: Line should read, "That swings the whole thing around—the actors become the audience and the audience becomes the actors."

137. 18th line from bottom: CUT: "I tell you it's a knockout." INSERT in its place: "It's the goddamndest play I ever saw in my life." (Balance of speech as is.)

139. 18th line from top: CORRECTION: Switch lines as follows:
Fanny: Oh, that's thrilling.
Gwen: Gives me gooseflesh.

140. 13th line from top: CORRECTION: Transpose Tony's line (& directions) "I think he's terrible" to immediately after Bert's line, "Well, what do you think of him?", up two speeches.

140. 15th line from bottom: CUT: "Here you are. Sit down." Also CUT directions: ("Fanny sits in her chair, her back to the audience").

140. 3rd line from bottom: CUT: "We've got to take him in by the fire, people."

141. 6th line from top: CORRECTION: 1st sentence should read: "Why shouldn't he?"

141. 12th line from top: CORRECTION: Should read: "Why shouldn't there be a scene where they carry on the baby?"

141. 18th line from top: INSERT: Julie's line to read: "Don't be silly, Gwen, he'll have to start some time."

141. 19th line from top: CORRECTION: Fanny's line should read, "Well of course he does!"

141. 14th line from bottom: CUT direction ("Gives glass to Fanny"), and sentence, "Here you are, Fanny!" Resume as follows:
Tony (holds aloft his glass): "Yeah, here's to the kid!"

141. 5th line from bottom: CORRECTION: After second "When one drops out," line should read:
". there will always be another"

141. 2nd line from bottom: CORRECTION: Fanny should say: "Aubrey Cavendish the Second."
All: "To Aubrey Cavendish the Second."
(They all drink).

142. 2nd line from top: After "Come on everybody . . ." CORRECTION: Next sentence should read, "Let's take him into the library."

142. 8th line from top: CORRECTION: Tony's speech should read: "Hey, everybody, you haven't heard the ballet music yet! How's the piano in there?"

142. 10th line from top: CORRECTION: Should read, "Are you coming, Mother?"

142. 11th line from top: CORRECTION: The sequence should go as follows:
(All exit but Fanny and Wolfe. He turns at library door and gives Fanny a hug.)
Fanny: "I'm so happy."
(Wolfe exits. The noise goes on from there, fainter, of course, but still heard, very merry. Tony is playing some gay strains on the off-stage piano. FANNY crosses towards piano, picks up her script, looks over photographs on piano, picks up one in particular—obviously of Aubrey—laughs lovingly, glances up at the portrait of Aubrey, replaces the photograph and turns the script to the opening pages. She moves about the stage searching for a way to make an "entrance." Finally mounts the staircase four or five steps, turns and begins to read silently, descends the stairs, saying the lines sotto voce. As she nears the chair, she has an attack, drops the script and falls into the chair.)

Note: From here, go to P. 142, 6th line from bottom, and follow as printed to CURTAIN. Also NOTE: Della's entrance and exit have been cut.

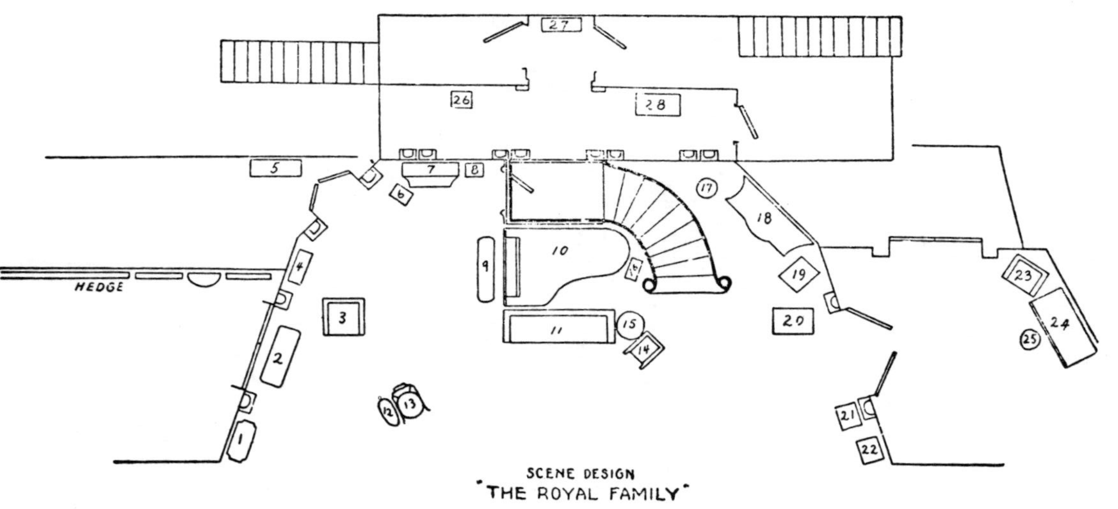

SCENE DESIGN
"THE ROYAL FAMILY"

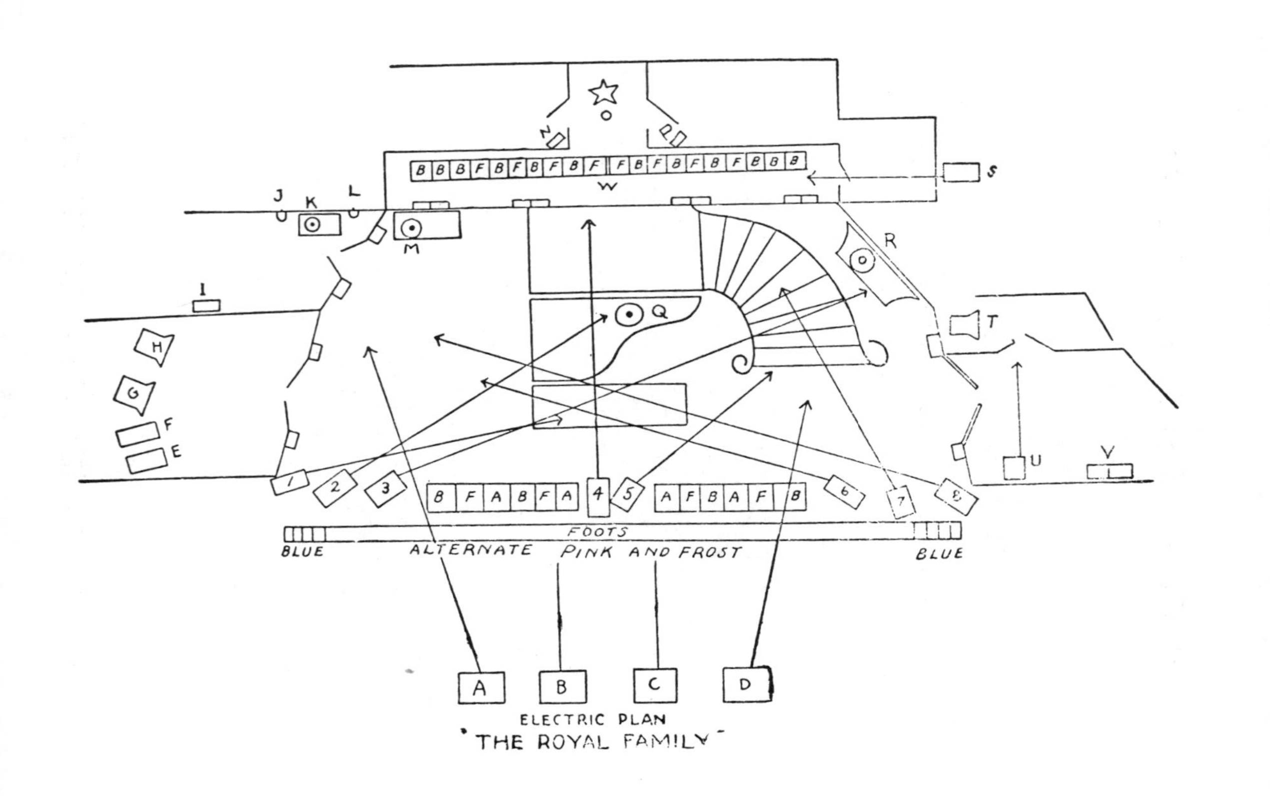

ELECTRIC PLAN
"THE ROYAL FAMILY"